Cambridge Elements

Elements in Evolutionary Economics
edited by
John Foster
University of Queensland
Jason Potts
RMIT University
Isabel Almudi
University of Zaragoza
Francisco Fatas-Villafranca
University of Zaragoza
David A. Harper
New York University

EVOLUTIONARY SELECTION AND KEYNES–SCHUMPETER MACROECONOMICS

Önder Nomaler
The United Nations University – Maastricht Economic and Social Research Institute on Innovation and Technology (UNU-MERIT)

Danilo Spinola
Birmingham City University

Bart Verspagen
Maastricht University

Shaftesbury Road, Cambridge CB2 8EA, United Kingdom

One Liberty Plaza, 20th Floor, New York, NY 10006, USA

477 Williamstown Road, Port Melbourne, VIC 3207, Australia

314–321, 3rd Floor, Plot 3, Splendor Forum, Jasola District Centre, New Delhi – 110025, India

103 Penang Road, #05–06/07, Visioncrest Commercial, Singapore 238467

Cambridge University Press is part of Cambridge University Press & Assessment, a department of the University of Cambridge.

We share the University's mission to contribute to society through the pursuit of education, learning and research at the highest international levels of excellence.

www.cambridge.org
Information on this title: www.cambridge.org/9781009619493

DOI: 10.1017/9781009619486

© Önder Nomaler, Danilo Spinola and Bart Verspagen 2025

This publication is in copyright. Subject to statutory exception and to the provisions of relevant collective licensing agreements, with the exception of the Creative Commons version the link for which is provided below, no reproduction of any part may take place without the written permission of Cambridge University Press & Assessment.

An online version of this work is published at doi.org/10.1017/9781009619486 under a Creative Commons Open Access license CC-BY-NC-ND 4.0 which permits re-use, distribution and reproduction in any medium for non-commercial purposes providing appropriate credit to the original work is given. You may not distribute derivative works without permission. To view a copy of this license, visit https://creativecommons.org/licenses/by-nc-nd/4.0

When citing this work, please include a reference to the DOI 10.1017/9781009619486

First published 2025

A catalogue record for this publication is available from the British Library.

ISBN 978-1-009-61949-3 Hardback
ISBN 978-1-009-61952-3 Paperback
ISSN 2514-3573 (online)
ISSN 2514-3581 (print)

Cambridge University Press & Assessment has no responsibility for the persistence or accuracy of URLs for external or third-party internet websites referred to in this publication and does not guarantee that any content on such websites is, or will remain, accurate or appropriate.

For EU product safety concerns, contact us at Calle de José Abascal, 56, 1°, 28003 Madrid, Spain, or email eugpsr@cambridge.org.

Evolutionary Selection and Keynes–Schumpeter Macroeconomics

Elements in Evolutionary Economics

DOI: 10.1017/9781009619486
First published online: September 2025

Önder Nomaler
The United Nations University – Maastricht Economic and Social Research Institute on Innovation and Technology (UNU-MERIT)

Danilo Spinola
Birmingham City University

Bart Verspagen
Maastricht University

Author for correspondence: Bart Verspagen, b.verspagen@maastrichtuniversity.nl

Abstract: This Element develops a stock-flow consistent agent-based macroeconomic model with Schumpeterian and Keynesian characteristics. On the Schumpeterian side, technological change is modelled as productivity growth as a result of research and development (R&D). The R&D strategies of firms are determined by an evolutionary selection process. On the Keynesian side, demand is endogenous on current income and the stock of households' financial wealth. In the long run, an evolutionary stable R&D strategy of firms emerges, leading to endogenous productivity growth. Demand adjusts endogenously to match labour-saving productivity growth, so that the employment rate is stationary, although with business cycle fluctuations. The authors use Monte Carlo simulations to analyze the emergence of an evolutionary stable R&D strategy, as well as the long-run properties of the model and the nature of business cycles. This title is also available as Open Access on Cambridge Core.

Keywords: Keynes-Schumpeter models, evolutionary agent-based economic models, innovation in macroeconomic models, demand-based growth models, evolutionary selection in economics

JEL classifications: E14, E12, E32, O30, O33, O40

© Önder Nomaler, Danilo Spinola and Bart Verspagen 2025

ISBNs: 9781009619493 (HB), 9781009619523 (PB), 9781009619486 (OC)
ISSNs: 2514-3573 (online), 2514-3581 (print)

Contents

1 Introduction   1

2 Background and Literature Review   5

3 Keynesian Economics: The Model for a Stationary Economy   13

4 Introducing R&D-Based Productivity Growth   34

5 Exploring the Full Model: Monte Carlo Simulations   53

6 Conclusions and Outlook   76

   Appendix I: The Steady State for a Notional Representative Agent   79

   Appendix II: List of Variables, Parameters and Parameter Settings   83

   References   86

1 Introduction

Schumpeter seemed not to have been impressed with the macroeconomic work of Keynes and the way it had found its way into the mainstream in the form of the so-called neoclassical synthesis (e.g., under the influence of Hicks, 1937). In his 1948 presidential address to the American Economic Association, he wrote about

> the absorption of Keynes' contribution into the current stream of analytic work [that t]here are no really new principles to absorb. The ideology of underemployment equilibrium and of non-spending – which is a better term to use than saving – is readily seen to be embodied in a few restrictive assumptions that emphasize certain (real or supposed) facts. With these everyone can deal as he thinks fit and for the rest he can continue his way. This reduces Keynesian controversies to the level of technical science. (Schumpeter, 1948, p. 356)

This is in stark contrast with the work of present-day neo-Schumpeterians (the work of some of which we will briefly review in Section 2), who see in Schumpeter and Keynes two kindred spirits as far as the deep nature of economic development as a disequilibrium process is concerned. Schumpeter viewed capitalism as a restless economic system, in which innovation (a supply-side factor) never allows equilibrium to settle. Keynes, on the other hand, saw demand-side factors, including the 'animal spirits' of entrepreneurs, leading to economic turbulence in the short- to middle-run, and was more interested in exploring the nature of those 'tempestuous seasons' than in the long-run equilibrium. We place ourselves in the neo-Schumpeterian scholarly tradition by insisting that macroeconomic dynamics result from interacting microeconomic agents instead of optimizing representative agents. Hence our contribution in this Element focuses on an agent-based view of macroeconomics, in which both Keynesian and Schumpeterian elements can be found.

Our main Schumpeterian message is that innovation is the driving force of economic growth and development, and that the endogenous emergence of innovation takes place as a process that is characterized by opportunity-seeking entrepreneurs who create innovation to escape the conditions of equilibrium (i.e., low profit rates) as dictated by competition. Much of the work in the Schumpeterian tradition has embraced the idea of bounded rationality, which defies the fully rational optimization strategies of standard microeconomics. Such bounded rationality still implies intentionality on the side of agents (innovating firms). We take a much more minimalistic approach, in which we assume no intentionality on the side of agents: each firm is assigned an R&D strategy (i.e., how much to invest in R&D relative to its sales revenue) and maintains that strategy throughout its lifetime, with the exception of occasional and purely random experimentation.

In this way, the burden for making the emergence of innovation possible lies at the system level, where economic selection decides on whether or not Research and Development (R&D) performing firms will survive. If R&D performing firms survive evolutionary selection, innovation leads to productivity growth. The absence of any degree of rationality for R&D performing firms is not intended as an approximation of how real firms work. Inspired by the ideas of evolutionary game theory, we use this assumption to show how interaction between agents alone can already create dynamic economic development as an emergent phenomenon.

The 'evolutionary game' nature of our model is implied by the fact that in the medium- to short-run, the survival chance of a firm is determined not only by the firm's own R&D strategy but also by those of other firms, which collectively shape the macroeconomic (selection) environment. The evolutionary nature of this process resides in the simultaneity of processes that generate variety (i.e., by random mutations of the firms' individual R&D strategies) and those that tend to eliminate the variety (i.e., selection implied by bankruptcies followed by stochastic imitation of the R&D strategies of better performers). Accordingly, one of the main aims of our analysis is to investigate whether this kind of selection can generate an outcome in which firms adopt an evolutionary stable R&D strategy (Maynard-Smith, 1974), leading to a situation where further experimentation with R&D strategies by firms does not lead the economy away from its growth path.

This 'evolutionary game' is set in a macroeconomic context with strong Keynesian features. Our Keynesian message is that demand does not adjust to supply in an automatic and smooth way. This requires the explicit modelling of demand and the interaction between demand and supply. Our choice here is to focus on an economy that can develop and grow without extensive government policy, whether aimed at the supply-side (e.g., innovation policy) or demand-side policy of the well-known Keynesian counter-cyclical kind.[1] Our aim is to sketch the basic elements of an economy that can grow without government intervention, although we do not expect such growth to be a smooth steady state.

The main Keynesian and Schumpeterian elements of our model can already be found in an earlier paper (Nomaler et al., 2021) that provides a purely aggregate version of the macroeconomic model that is used in this Element, although with two major limitations in the form of assumptions about

---

[1] Note that this is very different to other models in the Keynes–Schumpeter tradition (e.g., Dosi et al., 2010), which generally rely heavily on the government to provide demand, for example, in the form of unemployment benefits funded from tax income.

exogeneity. In that model, both R&D (and innovation) and the real wage rate (or the share of wages in GDP) are exogenous. However, this aggregate model provides the basic context of the interaction between demand and supply that is our version of the Keynes–Schumpeter synthesis that others in the neo-Schumpeterian field have also sought (see Section 2). In our version of Keynes–Schumpeter macroeconomics, innovation, as a supply-side factor, generates the potential for a long-run increase in living standards.

The realization of this potential depends on whether demand keeps pace with productivity growth. In Nomaler et al. (2021), this was achieved through the modelling of consumer demand as an endogenous fraction of households' financial wealth, which reacts to deviations of the (macro) employment rate from an assumed neutral level. In this way, households smooth their consumption levels when wage income fluctuates as a result of changes in the employment rate. This mechanism also enables the real wage rate, and hence consumer demand, to keep pace with productivity change.

Because this endogenization of demand plays an important role in the stock of financial wealth of households, the model needs to keep precise accounts of these stocks, including where in the economy the financial assets of households appear as liabilities. This is where we draw on the stock-flow consistent (SFC) macroeconomics of Godley and Lavoie (see, again, Section 2 for references and a brief overview). However, we adopt only the most simple and limited version of the SFC model, in which we do not explicitly model any banks, and the government sector has a completely passive role. This implies that in our model, households' financial wealth mostly corresponds to the debt of firms, and the government plays only a very modest role in demand. What we keep of the SFC ideas is that wealth/debt stocks that result cumulatively from past cash flows will affect the behaviour of the agents, thus what can happen in the current period. This introduces a process of 'circular cumulative causation' in the model.

The agent-based parts of the current model as well as the endogenization of the real wage rate draw on Meijers et al. (2019). This model is agent-based, as our current model is, but it does not have any growth. It provides elements of the selection environment that we will use in the current model, by portraying selection as closely connected to bankruptcy of firms that have become heavily indebted. This is the approach that we follow here as well, although, in the current model, R&D (which is absent in Meijers et al., 2019) is an important factor determining bankruptcy, as it relates both to productivity increases of the firm and represents a cost. The endogenization of the real wage rate is based on the idea that firms adjust their markup (of goods sold) to keep their leverage ratio (outstanding debt relative to the capital stock of the firm) within bounds (a high leverage ratio implies a high probability of going bankrupt).

What results in this Element is a macroeconomic model that presents the full view of our interpretation of the Keynes–Schumpeter synthesis. The model is agent-based, that is, it specifies how macroeconomic trends result from interacting agents without any assumption about rational behaviour as the basis for any of the main outcomes of the model, such as the emergence of growth and business cycles. The model is also fully endogenous; there are no important aspects left exogenous that determine the nature of the growth process or how growth arises from the interaction of demand and supply.

Our model is also relatively parsimonious, as it abstracts from the role of the government in demand stabilization and the role of the financial sector, both of which are factors that play a large role in other models, even within the Keynes–Schumpeter tradition. By this, we do not want to argue that the role of the government, the financial sector, or any other things that we abstract from are not important in the real-world economy. By keeping the model as simple as possible but still agent-based, we hope to provide a starting point for further analysis and also stay relatively close to the model in Nomaler et al. (2021).[2]

The rest of this Element is organized as follows. In Section 2 we will provide a brief outline of the literature that is immediately relevant for the construction and interpretation of our model. This includes a brief recount of the general nature of the Schumpeterian and Keynesian approaches to economic analysis, a short overview of some of the contributions of the Keynes–Schumpeter approach to macroeconomics, and a brief preview of our own model. Section 3 will specify the basics of our model, which means that it presents all aspects of the model except R&D and innovation. This comprises the Keynesian and stock-flow consistent (including balance sheets and the transaction table) sides of our model without the Schumpeterian part, that is, without R&D, and describes a stationary economy. We present some of the basic outcomes of this model in terms of simulations that generate business cycles.

In Section 4, we introduce R&D into the model. This starts with an analysis of the role that R&D plays in the cash flow equation of the firm and, hence, in the dynamics of debt of firms (and its reflection in household wealth). After this, we specify different innovation functions that provide a stochastic relation between firm-level R&D investment and innovation, which we model purely as productivity increases. Section 4 also makes use of the parsimonious nature of the model to derive a highly simplified ('representative agent') version of the model that allows us to treat R&D as exogenous and derive steady-state expressions for other important variables in the model that endogenously arise for different

---

[2] One difference between the model in Nomaler et al. (2021) and the current model is that the former is a supermultiplier model, while the current one has the 'normal' multiplier. We do not believe that this difference affects the results in any deep way.

levels of exogenous R&D. Simulations will show that by tweaking certain parameters, the fully agent-based model can approximate these 'exogenous R&D' steady states. This means that multiple growth paths are possible in the model, depending on what level of R&D is specified. We conclude Section 4 by identifying a set of parameter values with which the firm population can indeed adopt an evolutionary stable R&D strategy, which implies that a stable level of aggregate R&D emerges. In other words, while multiple levels of R&D investment are possible a priori, economic selection can pick one of them that is stable even if firms keep experimenting with mutated strategies.

Section 5 documents a number of simulation experiments, all of which are set up to yield evolutionary stable R&D strategies, in which we pick a small set of parameters to vary and analyze the variation in outcomes by Monte Carlo simulations. This includes an experiment about the emergence of R&D from a state of the model where no firm does any R&D, an experiment about the nature of the innovation process (how R&D influences the average waiting time and the size of innovations), an experiment about financial aspects of the economy that influence the selection environment, an experiment about the impact of the marginal propensity to consume, and an experiment about business cycles. Finally, in Section 6, we summarize the outcomes of the model and the implications they have for approaching macroeconomics from the Keynes–Schumpeter perspective. This will include a brief outline for a research agenda that elaborates on the simplifications of our model to more realistic settings.

2 Background and Literature Review

2.1 A Schumpeterian Disequilibrium Approach

The Schumpeterian view of the economic system rests on the principles of heterogeneity between agents and evolutionary dynamics. This is very different from what is found in the standard microeconomic textbooks, where behavioural homogeneity is the norm and representative agents are used to build economic theory. These different perspectives lead to conflicting views about the nature of economic dynamics, with a crucial role for the concept of economic equilibrium.

One definition of equilibrium, which also applies to the 'dynamic' idea of equilibrium as a steady state growth path (which is what interests us in this Element), is a state of the economic system in which no actor has an incentive for changing behaviour. In simple terms of demand and supply, this could mean that a price has been established at which buyers can buy everything they want, and at the same time, sellers are able to sell everything they want. Neither buyers nor suppliers have any reason to change their behaviour. In the textbook theory, such an equilibrium would be stated in terms of supply and demand curves, which are derived from profit maximization by a representative firm (the supply curve) and utility maximization by a representative consumer (the demand curve). At the price where these curves intersect, none of the agents will feel a need for change.

In the Schumpeterian perspective, the key assumption is that some agents will always want to inflict change upon any state of the economy, no matter how near it would be to the textbook equilibrium. Schumpeter takes a supply-side perspective and focuses on innovation as a way to disrupt the equilibrium. The Schumpeterian entrepreneur looks for profit opportunities beyond the profit rate that can be earned in equilibrium, that is, the 'above-normal' profits that the textbook models assume will be competed away. Innovation can create such profits as long as the innovating entrepreneur is not imitated on a large scale, that is, as long as she has some degree of exclusivity in the market.

If above-normal profits related to entrepreneurial, innovative activity exist for extended periods of time, then the textbook equilibrium can, in the best case, only be valid as a long-run target to which the economy may tend to move. This is the view expressed in Schumpeter's 1911 *Theorie der wirtschaftlichen Entwicklung*. The neo-Schumpeterian tradition that emerged in the 1980s (e.g., Mensch, 1979; Dosi, 1982; Freeman et al., 1982; Dosi et al., 1988) revived the theme of innovation as a disequilibrating force. In the closely related field of evolutionary economics (e.g., Nelson and Winter, 1982; Silverberg et al., 1988), economic selection was proposed as a way to formally model firms and the markets on which they operate as a selection process. Such an evolutionary view is fully compatible with the disequilibrium nature of the economy that Schumpeter proposed. It is also the tradition in which the model explored in this Element fits.

This neo-Schumpeterian evolutionary view of the economy developed in the same period that the so-called endogenous growth theory developed (e.g., Romer, 1990; Aghion and Howitt, 1992). Although this field, especially work following the original contribution by Aghion and Howitt, also refers to itself as neo-Schumpeterian, the approach there is based on equilibrium, and, hence, rather different from the neo-Schumpeterian evolutionary literature that we position ourselves in. In the endogenous growth theory, and contrary to Schumpeter's original view, innovation is an equilibrium process itself, for example, as in Romer's market for blueprints (inventions), where monopolistic competition rules and firms are able to charge an equilibrium markup over marginal costs.

While there is much to be said about these different interpretations of Schumpeter's ideas, we will not explore that topic in this Element. Instead, we are interested in developing a model that is characterized by Schumpeterian disequilibrium in an evolutionary context. Our emphasis will be on how evolutionary selection may lead to regularities in innovation rates at the level of the aggregate economy, and what this implies for economic growth. What we do share with the 'endogenous growth' approach of Romer, Aghion and Howitt is a focus on research and development (R&D) as a source of innovation, that is, the firm in our model will undertake R&D and, as a result, will have a probability of realizing an innovation.

R&D takes place at the microeconomic (firm) level, hence selection takes place between firms. The question of whether this selection process can lead to regularities at the microeconomic level, without the standard textbook equilibrium, fits in the questions addressed in the so-called complexity literature (e.g., Prigogine and Stengers, 1984; Silverberg, 1988; Langton, 1990). A central notion here is self-organization, which Silverberg (1988, p. 531) describes as follows:

> The theory of self-organization deals with complex dynamic systems open to their environment in terms of the exchange of matter, energy and information and composed of a number of interacting subsystems ... Many such systems have been shown ... to lead to the spontaneous emergence of coherent macroscopic structures ... from the seemingly uncoordinated behaviour of the component parts at the microscopic level. Moreover, self-organizing systems can undergo a succession of ... structural transformations.

The dominant approach to modeling selection at the microeconomic level has been to use a so-called replicator equation (e.g., Iwai, 1984a, b; Silverberg et al., 1988; Silverberg and Verspagen, 1994; Hofbauer and Sigmund, 1998). This equation describes how the market shares (or some other share variable that represents how an economic variable is distributed between firms) of firms change as a result of changes in so-called fitness. It is intended to capture Herbert Spencer's idea of 'survival of the fittest'; hence it requires an operationalization of what constitutes fitness. This could be profitability, product quality, or any other variable that would enhance firm performance. Firms that have higher (lower) fitness than the weighted average of all firms will see their market share increase (decline).

Our approach to selection is different. We follow the approach by Meijers et al. (2019), who model selection as the result of bankruptcy. Here, firms stay in the market as long as they have not gone bankrupt. Bankruptcy is a stochastic event, but its probability depends on the degree of indebtedness of the firm. While the basics of our model, and the bankruptcy-based selection process, are similar to Meijers et al., we introduce R&D and growth in the model. A major focus of the results that we will present here is how the R&D spending rate that a firm adopts influences the probability of bankruptcy. In other words, heterogeneity between firms in terms of their R&D strategies leads to different rates of survival, and the outcome of this selection process determines the aggregate rate of growth.

2.2 Keynes and the Role of Demand

The Schumpeterian perspective is dominated by the supply-side, with innovation playing a key role in generating disequilibrium. In contrast, in the work following the contributions of Keynes, demand-side factors are the source of disequilibrium. The combination of these two perspectives has led to a proposal for a 'Schumpeter–Keynes synthesis' (e.g., Dosi et al., 2010), which is indeed how we would position the contribution in this Element. Before we (briefly) discuss the Schumpeter–Keynes synthesis in the next section, this section illustrates how Keynesian tradition is relevant to our contribution.

The core idea behind Keynesian economics is often considered as a reaction to Say's law; that supply creates its own demand, even at the aggregate level. Keynes (1936) offered a strong critique of Say's law, noting that economic agents (e.g., households and capitalists) may choose to hold their wealth in liquid assets, such as cash.[3] This results in a leakage from the system, accumulating into a stock of assets that are, momentarily or for a longer term, withdrawn from the circular flow (i.e., from investment and/or consumption), and thus represents a lack of 'effective demand'. On the other hand, injections that are financed by debt or out of accumulated wealth can lead to excess demand. In this Keynesian view, not all (wage) income is necessarily consumed, nor is consumption always bound by current income. Investment reacts not to the availability of savings but to investors' expectations, their 'animal spirits', and the reward for liquidity, indicated by the interest rate.

Without supply-side domination, the relationship between spending and the macroeconomic outcome can be understood through the concept of the Keynesian multiplier, which is defined as the ratio of the change in aggregate income to an initial change in autonomous expenditure. Here, 'autonomous' means spending that is independent of current income, that is, spending that is not part of the complete and perfect circular flow as envisaged in Say's Law. To outline the role of the multiplier, we need to focus both on the working of the multiplier, and on the factors that determine autonomous demand.

---

[3] When one allows different types of monetary instruments and financial assets to enter the analysis, macroeconomic monetary aspects start to play an important role. We ignore such monetary considerations by making particular assumptions that simplify our model considerably. Therefore, we abstract from details of the monetary side of the Keynesian (or Schumpeterian) literature.

As Robinson (1937) stressed, the interplay between autonomous demand and the multiplier represents an alternative to the Walrasian general equilibrium way of macroeconomic coordination (see also Pasinetti, 2007). As argued earlier, consumption and investment plans of individual agents, including government, contain elements that are independent of current income (i.e., autonomous, financed ex ante by debt or out of accumulated wealth), and these plans are executed by microeconomic transactions (interaction) between agents. These interactions will induce production, and production will further induce consumption and investment (the latter represents the non-autonomous parts of investment and consumption).

For simplicity, we may assume that each (autonomous) euro spent initially by an economic agent leads to a euro worth of production that generates additional income for some household, and that in this way a fixed portion $\alpha < 1$ of the original euro is further spent. This α euro generates another fraction α additional spending, and so on, ad infinitum. Denoting total autonomous spending by A, aggregate income Y is then determined as the infinite series sum $Y = A(1 + \alpha + \alpha^2 + +\alpha^3 + \ldots + +\alpha^\infty)$, which, given $\alpha < 1$, converges to $Y = A \times 1/(1 - \alpha)$. The latter is the Keynesian Econ 101 expression for income determination by the multiplier: $1/(1 - \alpha)$ is the multiplier and A represents autonomous spending (e.g., investment, autonomous consumption and government spending). The 'propensity' parameter α will contain marginal spending out of current income, possibly differentiated by functional income category (wages and profits), as well as imports and tax payments (the latter two with a negative sign). The Sraffian supermultiplier tradition (e.g., Freitas and Serano, 2015) also considers investment as induced, and hence would include it in α.

The reduced-equation outcome of the multiplier process hides all of the complexity and variety that occurs in microeconomic interactions. Explicitly modelling these interactions, as we will venture in what follows in an agent-based modelling (ABM) context, is consistent with the self-organization principle as outlined earlier. The outcome of this process is one in which all production and consumption plans of individual agents have been simultaneously completed, adapted, coordinated and, ultimately, realized. It is also an outcome in which wealth has shifted between agents. Households or firms that accumulate a negative or positive cash flow over the entire multiplier process will see their net worth decline or increase, respectively. While the Schumpeterian side of the self-organizing economy stresses the role of supply-side factors such as innovation, the Keynesian perspective brings the demand-side into the analysis.

This is an inherently dynamic process, in which demand prompts producers to adjust their supply, thereby creating a dynamic interaction between demand and supply. Initial spending injections propagate through the economy in a dynamic way. In terms of autonomous demand, a large part of the body of Keynesian theory focuses on investment. This is where the 'animal spirits' described by Keynes play a pivotal role. Investors make decisions based on their expectations of future profitability, which are inherently uncertain and influenced by psychological factors (animal spirits). This reflects the confidence and optimism (or pessimism) that investors have about the future, driving their willingness to undertake new investments. High expectations of future returns encourage investment, stimulating economic activity and growth. Conversely, low expectations can lead to reduced investment and economic stagnation. It is common to assume in the Keynesian literature that these expectations are largely myopic, for example, that firms make investment plans on the basis of their current rate of capacity utilization (i.e., the 'accelerator model' of investment). Such feedbacks from the current state of the economy to expectations gives rise to another dynamic process in the multiplier process, which increases the probability of low-activity (high unemployment) attractors in the system.

In this way, the multiplier process is a double-edged sword in terms of macroeconomic coordination. It has the potential to destabilize the economy by magnifying exogenous shocks to autonomous demand (given myopic expectations), but also to help the (re)stabilization by magnifying the due changes in autonomous demand that results as a 'corrective' response to divergences from potential output. This leads to one of the basic (but also controversial as seen by the mainstream) ideas of Keynesian economics, which is that government policy may use this dynamic process to stabilize the economy. When demand is too low as evidenced by high unemployment and low activity levels, an increase in government spending stimulates demand, which will have a disproportionately large effect through the multiplier. Conversely, in times of economic overheating, the multiplier can help moderate demand through taxation and reduced government spending, thereby preventing inflationary pressures. Recent studies have documented this dynamic nature of fiscal multipliers and their implications for macroeconomic stability (Taylor, 2020; Arestis & Sawyer, 2004).

2.3 Schumpeter and Keynes: A Preview of Our Approach

There are a variety of approaches to the Keynes–Schumpeter synthesis. Most of them are either set in a context of sectoral models of structural change (e.g., Lorentz et al., 2016), or explicitly stated in terms of complex interactive systems, particularly ABMs. Agent-based models are focused on the interactions of heterogeneous agents – households, firms and banks – each following its behavioural rules. These interactions lead to emergent macroeconomic phenomena, such as the multiplier effect. In ABMs, the decision-making processes of individual agents, such as consumption, saving and investment, can be directly modelled to observe how they contribute to aggregate demand. This approach allows for exploring how micro-level behaviours and interactions lead to macroeconomic outcomes, capturing the complexity and dynamism of the real economy. By modelling the economy from the bottom up, ABMs provide insights into the micro-foundations of the multiplier effect, revealing how individual actions collectively influence macroeconomic stability and growth.

Dosi et al. (2010) present a Schumpeter–Keynes model in which the Schumpeterian side is represented by a capital goods sector that searches, by R&D, for new machines that have higher labour productivity (Tesfatsion, 2002). These machines are sold to a consumer goods sector. In the consumer goods sector, firms' market shares evolve according to a replicator equation, which is the main evolutionary ingredient of the model. The Keynesian side of the model is represented by the use of adaptive expectations about demand, the investment equation in which investment responds to capacity utilization, and by a government that provides unemployment benefits to workers who do not find jobs. On the other hand, the model also assumes that all wage income is consumed in the current period, thus leaving no role for autonomous consumption demand or the accumulation of wealth by workers.

The model is calibrated to produce results that mimic empirical micro- and macroeconomic phenomena, such as a sustained positive growth rate along with business cycle fluctuations in output, and firm size and firm growth distributions. However, without Keynesian demand policies (i.e., unemployment benefits), the economy tends to get trapped in a state of unreasonably high unemployment rates. This crucial role of public spending as a stabilizer that smooths out microeconomic supply shocks arising from labour productivity gains is the main Keynesian feature of the model that the authors underline.

Caiani et al. (2014) propose an alternative Keynes–Schumpeter ABM, in which they put a lot of emphasis on the monetary side of the economy. Their model is explicitly based on the so-called SFC modelling tradition, with a large role for the financial market in facilitating investment as well as innovation. The setting of the model is one in which innovative entrepreneurs (who sell new machines that can be used in the consumer goods sector) 'invade' the market and push out sellers of traditional machines. This captures the Schumpeterian disequilibrium dynamics (Schumpeter, 1911) that were pointed to earlier.

Also in our own approach, the stock-flow-consistent (SFC) modelling tradition of Godley and Lavoie (2007) plays a major role in representing the Keynesian side, because this provides an intuitive way to endogenize (a part of) autonomous demand. In our implementation of the SFC model, consumption demand depends both on current wage income (with a propensity to consume that is < 1) and on the stock of wealth of households. The latter is an important part of autonomous demand (investment and R&D are the other parts), while the former represents induced demand. The accounting framework ensures that the aggregate wealth of households is equal to the aggregate debt of the firms (and the government) and that savings are equal to investment ex-post (as an identity). We model the simplest possible financial sector in which households hold firm and government bonds. Thus, our SFC framework accounts for the interactions between different sectors of the economy – households, firms and the financial sector. Intertemporal consumption smoothing by households (the propensity to consume out of the accumulated wealth in response to the employment rate) suffices for the emergence of sustained economic growth that closely follows aggregate labour productivity. Unlike the case of Dosi et al. (2010), the model does not require government (fiscal) policies in order not to be trapped in a state of mass unemployment, thanks to the consumption smoothing response of the individual households to unemployment.

In addition to being SFC, our approach is also partially ABM. The agent-based nature of our approach follows from two main aspects of the model. First, our implementation literally mimics the multiplier process, as described earlier, in a distributed way. Individual households and firms make bilateral transactions with (other) individual firms, both in the goods and the labour market. This starts with the exercise of autonomous demand (by households and firms) and continues until all demand, including induced demand that results endogenously in the process, is satisfied, or, exceptionally, rationing takes place due to supply constraints. All goods transactions lead to immediate production and hence labour demand, and each transaction is a cash flow from the buyer to the seller (i.e., a firm that hires a fractional unit of the household's labour or a household that purchases a fractional unit of the good produced by the firm); thus, an increment to the wealth stock of the latter comes at the cost of an equal reduction in the wealth stock of the former.

The other agent-based part of our model is R&D, where each firm has a particular R&D strategy that specifies how much it spends as a fraction of its total sales. A firm is born with an R&D strategy, which it can only change by low-probability random mutation or by the imitation if the firm is re-born after bankruptcy. Although we believe that, in actual reality, firms change R&D strategy endogenously, we adopt this simple approach to bring out the evolutionary nature of our model in an extreme and pure way. Here, the main question is whether selection will lead to stable and relatively homogenous R&D strategies in the firm population.

Because R&D leads to innovation (this is a stochastic process) in the form of labour productivity growth, and more R&D leads to larger and/or more innovations, the outcome of the selection process has implications for economic growth. Thus, the Schumpeterian innovation logic is the leading factor that determines growth in our model. On the other hand, the Keynesian multiplier process and its SFC implementation ensure that, in the long run, capacity utilization and employment rates remain within reasonable bounds. The basics of this mechanism, but with exogenous R&D spending, were already shown to produce a potentially stable steady state in the single-agent approach of Nomaler et al. (2021). Our current model endogenizes R&D as an evolutionary selection outcome.

It is important to emphasize that the ways in which the R&D spending rate that a firm adopts influences the probability of bankruptcy is not independent of the R&D spending by other firms. For instance, a firm spending very little on R&D may fare well as long as most other firms are also spending little, and, as a result, the economy is stagnant. However, a firm spending very little on R&D (and hence realizing almost no productivity growth) when most other firms are spending much and hence economizing on labour costs may face bankruptcy because wages are keeping up with productivity. This interdependence of the success of R&D strategies gives our model its evolutionary game flavor that makes notion of evolutionary stability a key question in assessing model outcomes.

In summary, in our Keynes–Schumpeter implementation, autonomous demand in the form of selection-determined R&D, investment (Keynesian animal spirits), and consumption partially based on accumulated wealth leads to current-period cash flows that play out through the multiplier process. In turn, these cash flows accumulate into next-period stocks (of debt, wealth and capital), which are the cumulative outcome of the flows of the past. This is a particular implementation of the process of circular cumulative causation that plays a large role both in various flavours of the Keynesian literature (e.g., Berger, 2009) as well as in the Schumpeterian growth literature (e.g., Fagerberg et al., 2021).

The details of this process will be discussed in the sections that follow.

3 Keynesian Economics: The Model for a Stationary Economy

We start by describing the Keynesian side of our model. The core of this is an agent-based (i.e., decentralized) multiplier process, which 'coordinates' the economy by equating demand and supply in the short run. Given the wage rate, the multiplier process generates the financial flows that accumulate into stocks (generally debt for firms and accumulated wealth for households) that are used to endogenize demand. We also describe the wage-setting process, which results from an endogenous markup that depends on the leverage ratio of the firm. These elements describe a Keynesian macroeconomy that has no growth but only short-run business cycle fluctuations. We will illustrate these business cycles by some simulations that will conclude the section.

The short-run specification of our model is very similar to the model in Meijers et al. (2019). In this section, we briefly summarize the equations and mechanisms of this part of the model. In the next section, we focus on selection and R&D, and explain how the model has a 'notional' steady-state attractor for the short-run dynamics.

There are three types of agents in the model: firms, households and a government. There is a market for a homogenous good produced by firms, a market for labour, and a rudimentarily modelled financial market. For simplicity, we assume that labour is also homogenous, and can be used to perform R&D and goods interchangeably. Households supply labour, consume, and hold a stock of financial wealth that results from past savings. Firms produce the homogenous good, using a capital stock and labour. The homogenous good can either be consumed or invested. Consumption depends on current income as well as the wealth of households. The only role for the government is to supply bonds, which is one type of asset in which households can invest their savings, and to try to achieve a balanced budget where tax income is equal to interest payments on bonds.

3.1 Time and the Multiplier Process

The short-run time scale of the model is organized around the Keynesian multiplier. Over a single period of the model (we roughly think about a period as a quarter, for reasons that we will discuss in the next section), the multiplier process starts fresh, unfolds itself in an iterative process, and ultimately finishes when demand is equal to supply. This process consists exclusively of transactions in the goods market and the labour market. It leads to changes in the stock of wealth of households and the stock of capital of firms, and determines activity levels (capital utilization and the employment rate) of the macro economy.

We can use the metaphor of a physical marketplace to explain this multiplier process. When the market opens, sellers of the homogenous good await buyers, who arrive with a fixed set of plans about how much (in terms of units of the homogenous good) they want to purchase. These buyers are both firms, who want to buy the homogenous good for investment purposes, and households, who are buying for consumption. Firms also come with autonomous demand in the form of their R&D plans. They have a fixed budget for R&D every period, which is spent similarly to the way investment plans are realized, that is, by purchasing the homogenous good from randomly selected firms).

These initial purchase plans are the autonomous part of demand, that is, these plans are independent of income in the period that is about to unfold. Autonomous consumption depends on the wealth stock of households, investment plans depend on past capacity utilization, and R&D plans result from the firm's R&D strategy (equations for the formation of the components of autonomous will be specified in what follows).

Transactions take place when buyers are selected randomly (as long as they are willing to buy) and matched randomly to sellers (as long as they are willing to sell). Firms that have higher unused capacity are more likely to be selected by a buyer. The price of goods is a numeraire, that is, it is equal to one in all goods transactions. Investment demand is served with priority (before all other demand), so that firms can (likely) realize their investment plans without rationing (note that investment goods produced at period t are added to the firm's capital stock only at period $t+1$). The goods that exchange hands in these transactions are produced on the spot, and, therefore, lead to a labour transaction (firms hire the labour necessary to produce the desired quantity on the spot). A sales tax is also paid on the spot. The labour transactions yield wage income, of which a part is saved and another part gives rise to new demand for goods (the latter is the induced part of household consumption). Induced consumption (which is the only part of demand that depends on current income) is added to the consumption plans of households, thus fuelling the multiplier process that is unfolding in the marketplace. All transactions take place in very small batches, that is, it takes many transactions (with different agents in each small transaction) to fulfil total demand by one agent. In other words, both the demand for goods and for labour are allocated among the agents fractionally.

Because the household's marginal propensity to consume out of current wage income is smaller than one, total demand in the marketplace will tend to die out. When total unsatisfied demand falls below a (very small) threshold, the market is closed, the multiplier process is finished, and the period ends.[4] At this point, the financial side of all transactions is aggregated, resulting in a surplus or

---

[4] We allow for the possibility that rationing needs to take place because there is not enough capital or labour available to produce any remaining demand. This leaves unsatisfied demand and in the next period, the economy continues with the stocks that resulted after rationing. This happens only with specific parameter settings, which we avoid in the results that are presented in what follows.

deficit (or, on rare occasions, balance) for each agent. When savings out of current wage income are larger (smaller) than autonomous consumption, the household will have a surplus (deficit), and when the cash flow of a firm is negative (positive), its debt will increase (decrease). The sum of these deficits and surpluses over the entire economy will always be zero.

The financial market will settle the surpluses and deficits: agents with a current surplus will lend to agents with a deficit, and interest is paid over these loans. We do not model this financial sector in detail, and instead follow the simplest case in Godley and Lavoie (2007), where the government sets an exogenous interest rate on its bonds, which it supplies in a completely elastic way. Firms pay a spread over the interest rate on government bonds to compensate for the risk of bankruptcy, in which they forego part of their outstanding debt.

When the multiplier market process is closed, and all financial transactions have been accounted for, the longer timescale of the model kicks in to adapt the structure of the economy. This is when bankruptcies and entry take place (heavily indebted firms are replaced by fresh entrants), innovation takes place (based on their R&D investments, firms participate in a lottery for productivity improvements), firms update their investment plans, and possibly their R&D strategy, households update their (individual) propensity to consume out of wealth, and the government updates the tax rate to try to pursue a balanced budget. With all these structural changes, the economy enters a new multiplier period.

We now specify the equations and procedures that represent the details of this process.

3.2 Transactions and Matching

Buyers and sellers in transactions (both for goods and for labour) are drawn randomly, and transactions take place in small batches, which implies that each household or firm has transactions with a large range of other agents within a single period. We first draw a buyer randomly, and this buyer gets to buy a small quantity γ of goods. The actual purchase that this agent will make is equal to $G = min(\gamma, Z)$ where γ is the standard batch size, and Z is the total purchase that the agent still wants to make. The price of the homogenous good is always equal to 1, or, in other words, this price is a numeraire. As a result, this price plays no role in our model, and the goods market has to be cleared by the multiplier process alone.

The buying agent randomly selects a seller, where each seller (firm) has a probability of being selected that depends on how much it has already sold (produced) in the current period, relative to its capital stock. To define this

Keynes–Schumpeter Macroeconomics

probability, we first define the short-run utilization rate $\varsigma_j = q_j/Q_j^K$ for firm j, where q_j is total sales (production) of j in the period so far, and Q_j^K is full capacity output of the firm in the period (we will formally define Q_j^K later). We then calculate

$$\varsigma_j^* = (\varsigma_j - \varsigma^{min}) / (\varsigma^{max} - \varsigma^{min}) \text{ and } \varsigma_j^{**} = \min\left(1, \max\left(\varsigma_j^*, 0\right)\right).$$

The probability of the firm being selected as a seller is equal to the share of that firm in the sum of all ς_j^{**}. In this way, demand for goods will be distributed over firms in a way that is close to the distribution of capital over firms.

In the labour market, every household offers one unit of labour every period. When firms are in demand for labour, they buy in small batch sizes of ϵ units of labour, and they select a random household to employ for this amount. All households have an equal probability of being selected, except those who have already supplied $\varepsilon > 1$ units. Here, ε is a parameter that poses a harsh limit on total employment in the economy (it is larger than 1 to represent overwork). If all households supply ε units of labour, the economy becomes constrained and rationing needs to take place. The amount of labour exchanged in a single transaction is equal to $H = min(\epsilon, U)$, where U is the amount of labour that the supplying household can still supply before reaching ε.

All workers will get a wage rate that is a fraction σ of average productivity, that is, if $\bar{a}_t$ represents average productivity in production, then the economy-wide wage rate paid to production workers is $w_t = \bar{a}_t \sigma_{t-1}$. The variable σ_t is the share of wages in production value added, and is an important regulator of the economy that we will discuss in what follows.

In every transaction, the bank accounts of the involved parties are changed. For transactions in the goods markets, the buyer pays $G(1 + \tau)$, the seller gets G and the government gets τG. In a labour market transaction, no taxes are involved, so the buying firm pays Hw and the selling household gets the same amount.

3.3 Autonomous Spending

Autonomous spending has three components: investment in fixed capital by firms, R&D expenditures by firms, and the autonomous part of household consumption. We will now present the equations for these three components, starting with autonomous household consumption. Autonomous consumption spending by household j is denoted by Z_j^h and it evolves as follows:

$$Z_{jt}^h = \zeta_{jt} W_{jt}/(1 + \tau).$$

Here W_j is the stock of monetary wealth of the household, τ is the sales tax rate (set by the government), and ζ_{jt} is a household-level dynamic variable for consumption smoothing. $\zeta_j W_j$ represents nominal spending in monetary units. Firms charge a fixed price of 1 per unit of the homogenous good, so that $1 + \tau$ is the price paid by the household.

This consumption smoothing variable was introduced by Nomaler et al. (2021) at the macro-level. It captures the idea that households use autonomous consumption to smooth their consumption if wage income fluctuates with the employment rate. The consumption smoothing variable ζ_j varies in response to the household's own employment rate:

$$\zeta_{jt+1} = \zeta_{jt} + \alpha\left(\overline{E} - \widetilde{E}_{jt}\right),$$

where $\overline{E}$ is a desired employment rate that is common to all households. Remember that, due to the way the multiplier process works, individual households are fractionally employed, that is, their employment rate E_{jt} is a fractional rather than a binary number. $\widetilde{E}_{jt}$ is the household's average employment rate over the last T^E periods (we use $T^E = 5$), and α is a parameter. Thus, if the household's employment rate $\widetilde{E}_{jt}$ falls below (rises above) the target employment rate $\overline{E}$, they will use a larger (smaller) fraction of their financial wealth for consumption. This has a stabilizing effect. For the differential equation model of Nomaler et al. (2021), exact conditions for a stable employment rate equal to $\overline{E}$ can be derived. In the simulation results that we discuss in this Element, we see some fluctuations around such a stable employment rate.

Consumption-smoothing as specified in the preceding equation will be a crucial element of the model when growth gets introduced in the next section. In the context of the Meijers et al. (2019) model, ζ was a parameter. Growing productivity as a result of innovation will tend to create technological unemployment, and with ζ as a fixed parameter, this will either make the unemployment rate go to 100%, when demand does not keep up because ζ is too low (high), or lead to rationing of aggregate production by labour if ζ is too high. Varying ζ as a result of consumption smoothing prevents this and keeps the economy on a path where unemployment (or demand for labour) does not become very high. In other words, the feasibility of a Schumpeterian growth path depends crucially on this demand-side (hence Keynesian) process of consumption smoothing. This is a very crucial element of our Keynes–Schumpeter synthesis.

Investment plans of firm i depend on its pre-existing capital stock and its capital utilization rate:

$$I_{i,t} = \max\left(0, \delta K_{i,t-1} + K_{i,t-1}\varphi(u_{i,t-1} - \bar{u})\right),$$

where I is investment, K is the capital stock, δ is the depreciation rate of capital, u is the capital utilization rate, $\bar{u}$ is the 'neutral' capacity utilization rate (with $u = \bar{u}$, the firm invests just enough to match depreciation, that is, to keep the capital stock constant) and φ is a parameter that represents adjustment flexibility of investment. Both I and K are in units of the homogenous good. We assume a constant capital-to-output ratio given by the parameter ν, that is, at 'full' (or normal) capacity, ν units of capital provide capacity to produce 1 unit of the homogenous good). Accordingly, the capital utilization rate is computed as actual output divided by output at full utilization capital:

$$u \equiv \frac{Q}{Q^K}, Q^K \equiv \frac{K}{\nu},$$

where Q is output and Q^K is full-capacity output. As mentioned earlier, investment purchased in period t is added to the capital stock of the firm only at period $t+1$, after depreciation is accounted for:

$$K_{i,t} = K_{it-1}(1 - \delta) + I_{it-1}.$$

The final component of autonomous spending is R&D. As already mentioned, the autonomous R&D budget is spent on purchases of the homogenous good. Each firm has an R&D strategy parameter, which is assigned at its birth and which can only change due to occasional random mutation. Similarly to Silverberg and Verspagen (1994), the R&D strategy parameter specifies the fraction of total production (sales) that the firm spends on R&D. For firm i we have

$$R_{it} = \rho_{i,t} Q_{it-1},$$

where R is the R&D budget of the firm and ρ is the firm's R&D strategy variable. At each period t, the firm spends this amount autonomously to buy R_{it} units of the homogenous good. In this section, we will assume $\rho_{i,t} = 0$, while in the next section we will specify how mutation may change the R&D strategy over time and how R&D impacts on the innovation result of the firm.

3.4 The Financial Market

At the end of each period, some agents will be left with a surplus (e.g., a household that spent less on autonomous consumption than its savings from income in the period), and others with a deficit (e.g., a firm that spent more on investment and R&D than its operational surplus from production). Following the SFC tradition, our model keeps track of the accumulated accounts of these surpluses and deficits, which represent stocks of wealth or debt. For a viable economy (circular flow or growth path) to exist, firms need to accumulate a collective debt, and households need to hold this debt in the form of financial wealth. As already explained, the financial wealth of households impacts their consumption spending. The accumulated debt of firms puts an important constraint on their behaviour, as will be explained in the next section.

In light of our aim for a parsimonious model, our modelling of the financial market uses a very simple setup. In particular, we abstract from introducing the many types of financial assets that many in the SFC use, following the pioneering work of Godley and Lavoie (2007). For instance, we do not explicitly model a banking sector, which implies there is no credit-rationing (i.e., firms can borrow as much as they can by issuing interest-bearing bonds). Likewise, we assume away equity and dividend payments.

We use only two types of assets, both of which are bonds. One type of bond is issued by the government and is risk-free, while the other kind of bond is issued by firms. Private bonds[5] are risky, because the issuer may go bankrupt, and in this case, the holder of the bonds suffers a financial loss. Therefore, private bonds must pay a risk premium above the interest rate on government bonds. All bonds are perpetual, but the issuer may buy them back, according to their current credit needs and means.

The outstanding (cumulative) debt (i.e., bonds issued) by firm i is denoted by B_{it}. The convention is that B is a positive number if the firm has a debt. Firms pay an interest rate r^B to the holders of the bond, and this interest is paid at the beginning of the next period. We do not track which households hold how many bonds of which firms. For convenience, we assume that the portfolio of the bonds held by each household (who are heterogenous in their individual wealth) are identical in terms of the shares of the bonds. This means that when a firm goes bankrupt, the wealth accordingly lost by each household is proportional to their share in total wealth.

Interest payments are part of the cash flow of the firm, and hence, they accumulate new debt, whereas, on the side of the holding households, interest accrues to their financial wealth stock. In this way, the debt of the firm evolves as follows:

$$B_{i,t} - B_{i,t-1} = r^B_{t-1} B_{i,t-1} + I_{i,t} + R_{i,t} - \Pi_{i,t},$$

---

[5] One can see the private bonds as a combination of bonds and loans, but due to the lack of an explicit banking sector in the model, we refer to all outstanding debt of firms as bonds for simplicity.

where $\Pi_i = Q_i(1 - {w_t}/{a_i})$ is the operational surplus from production (sales minus labour compensation), and a_j is the firm's labour productivity. The right-hand side of this equation represents the cash flow of the firm, which will play an important role in the next section.

Besides the bonds issued by firms, households have a choice of buying bonds issued by the government, denoted by B^G, which pay an interest rate r^G, exogenously set. Government bonds are issued in a completely elastic way, that is, whatever amount of government bonds is demanded by households is what is supplied by the government.

The share of private bonds that household j wants to hold is determined as follows:

$$\frac{B_j}{W_j} = \max\left(0, \min\left(1, 1 - \theta_0 + \theta_1\left(r^B - r^G\right)\right)\right),$$

where $\theta_0, \theta_1 > 0$ are parameters. There is one equation like this for every household, and the sum of all of these (over all households) represents aggregate demand for firm bonds. From the aggregate perspective, r^B is the only unknown in this collection of equations values. The government will supply as many government bonds as are needed to fill the gap between aggregate household wealth and aggregate household demand for firm bonds. Aggregate values for B (total firm bonds held by household) and W (total household wealth) result from the transactions in the past period. All this implies that we can solve numerically over all households for r^B. Larger (smaller) values of θ_1 will yield a smaller (larger) interest rate spread $r^B - r^G$.

3.5 Bankruptcy

Bankruptcy is the way in which the selection of firms and their R&D strategies will take place in the full model that results after we introduce innovation in the next section. The detailed description of the economic selection mechanism that is connected to bankruptcy, that is, the way in which bankruptcy gives rise to retention of some R&D strategies, destroys others and introduces novelty in the R&D strategy space, is given in the next section. Here, we explain how bankruptcy leads to the death of a firm (which is followed by the birth of a new one). The cause of bankruptcy is an excessive amount of debt that the firm accumulates. This is measured by the leverage ratio of the firm, which is the ratio of outstanding debt (bonds issued) to the capital stock, which represents the total value of the firm. The net worth of firm j is $K_j - B_j$ and the leverage ratio is $b_j = B_j/K_j$.

The bankruptcy event is stochastic. When the leverage ratio of the firm rises above a threshold b^{lo}, this probability becomes positive (below b^{lo} it is zero). The bankruptcy probability rises in a linear fashion up to the point where the leverage ratio becomes b^{hi} and the bankruptcy probability becomes 1 (and stays 1 above b^{hi}).

We allow the bankruptcy probability to be influenced by other factors than firm debt, in particular by the relative productivity of the firm. In this way, 'better' (i.e., more productive) firms have more lenience from bond holders, allowing them to become somewhat more indebted than an otherwise similar firm. The lower bankruptcy limit then becomes firm-specific and equal to

$$b^{lo}_{jt} = b^{lo} + min\left(\left(\frac{a_{jt}}{\bar{a}_t} - 1\right)\tilde{b}, (b^{hi} - b^{lo})\check{b}\right),$$

where $\tilde{b}$ and $\check{b}$ are parameters, a_{jt} is firm j's (labour) productivity, and $\bar{a}_t$ is economy-wide labour productivity, both at period t, and b^{lo} (without firm or time subscript) remains the same parameter as before. The productivity effect on bankruptcy probability has an upper limit given by the min() expression. Note that if we set $\tilde{b} = 0$, the first term in the min() expression becomes zero and prevails over the second term (which is positive). In other words, $\tilde{b} = 0$ switches the productivity effect on bankruptcy off.

If a firm goes bankrupt, it goes out of business and is replaced by a new firm. This is the only way that firm entry happens in the model. The new firm takes over the capital stock of the bankrupt firm, but due to adjustment costs, it has to forego a fraction η, that is, it 'inherits' $(1 - \eta)K_j$ of the bankrupt firm j. The re-born firm does not inherit the full debt of the bankrupt firm. Instead, it inherits a debt that is equal to χK_j, where j refers to the bankrupt firm, and $\chi < 1$ is a parameter. This means that households take a loss to their financial wealth that is equal to $(1 - \chi)K_j$. This loss is distributed over all private bond holders (mostly households, but also firms and the government may hold private bonds) in proportion to their wealth (i.e., we assume that all bond holders are exposed equally to bankruptcy). Note that $\chi < b^{lo}$, which we have in all simulations, puts the new-born firm in a safe zone with respect to a new bankruptcy.

There are also arrangements for what happens with the R&D strategy of a new-born firm, but these will be discussed in the next section.

Although this happens relatively rarely, households may also become indebted individually (i.e., their wealth becomes negative), and the model allows households to write private bills just as firms write them. Indebted households pay interest on these outstanding bills, which are treated just the same as firm bills in the interest-setting process. Households can also go bankrupt, in the same stochastic way that firms go bankrupt. In this case, the variable that determines the bankruptcy probability, that is, the household equivalent of the leverage ratio, is the household's debt over the average production wage rate in the economy, that is, $-W_{jt}/w_t$ (only if $W_{jt} < 0$). The thresholds are bh^{lo} and bh^{hi}. When a household goes bankrupt, its complete debt is forgiven and deducted from holders of private bonds.

3.6 Government

As was already explained earlier, the government pays interest on the government bonds that other agents hold. In order to finance these interest payments, it raises a sales tax on all goods transactions. The government is willing to run a deficit, that is, to pay more interest than what it receives from the sales tax, but this cumulative deficit is targeted at a fixed proportion of the economy's productive capacity (i.e., the capital stock). Specifically, the government adjusts the sales tax rate as follows:

$$\tau_t = \min\left(\tau_{t-1} + \check{d}\left(\frac{\Delta_{t-1}}{K_{t-1}} - \vartheta\right), \tau^{max}\right),$$

where $\check{d}$ and ϑ are parameters, and Δ is the accumulated deficit of tax income minus interest payments of the government. The sales tax is not allowed to rise above a threshold τ^{max}.

Obviously, this specifies a very minor role for the government. In particular, we assume that the government has no active stabilization policy aimed at taming the business cycle. This is, again, a result of our desire for parsimoniousness. The agents (households and firms) in the economy described by our model, be it the stagnant one of this section or the growing one of the next section, will be able to grow by themselves, without the intervention of a government that needs to take account of a sufficient level of demand.

3.7 The Stock-Flow Nature of the Model

To summarize the exact nature of stocks and flows in the model, we present Tables 1 and 2, which, respectively, specify the balance sheets of agent groups, and the transaction table. We follow the conventions in Godley and Lavoie (2007) to set up these tables, but our versions are much simpler than theirs, because, as already explained, our model abstracts from many factors and processes that are modelled in detail in the SFC tradition.

Table 1 shows that total assets in the economy are equal to the capital stock of production firms, K. This is owned jointly by households, firms and the government. The capital stock is an asset held by firms,[6] hence it appears with a positive sign in the column for firms. The liabilities of

---

[6] We assume away equity, for this would unnecessarily complicate the model in ways that would require the compartmentalization of the households into a worker and a capitalist class.

Table 1 Balance sheets

Balance sheet items	Households	Firms (current)	Government	Sum
Capital stock	0	+K	0	+K
Government bonds	$+B^G$	0	$-B^G$	0
Private bonds	+B	−B	0	0
Net worth	$-NW_H$	$-NW_F$	$-NW^G$	−K
Sum	0	0	0	0

firms (negative sign in the column for firms) consist of outstanding firm bonds B and the net worth of the firm, NW_F. Household assets consist of financial holdings, or bonds, which consist of firm bonds (B) and government bonds, B^G. The sum of these two types of bonds is the net worth of households, NW_H, which is the same as the financial wealth stock of households that they use to smooth their consumption as modelled by the household-level variable ζ.

The limited role that we specify for the government implies that it has no assets, only liabilities in the form of outstanding government bonds (B^G). Hence, the net worth of the government, NW_G, will be negative (if other agents hold government bonds). The sum of net worth over all three types of agents is equal to the capital stock of firms. Because all transactions are directly credited and debited to the accounts in the balance sheet, there is no cash money or bank money.

Table 2 shows the transaction matrix for one period. Typically, firms produce the exact amount of goods that they need to serve total demand, which consists of consumption demand (C), investment (I) and R&D (R). This is illustrated on the first three rows of the transaction matrix, where these three variables enter with a positive sign in the current account column of firms. In these transactions, the buyers also pay the consumption tax, hence, these expenditures are multiplied by $(1 + \tau)$ when they enter as an expenditure (a negative sign) in the household column (consumption) or investment and R&D in the capital account of firms. The portion of tax in each of these transactions enters as income (hence a positive sign) in the government column.

Firms pay wages to households, and the total of this is equal to the wage rate ($w = \sigma \times a$, where σ is the wage share, specified in the next section, and a is the economy-wide labour productivity, which will be endogenized in the next section). Depreciation of capital (δK) enters as a cost to firms that is subtracted in the calculation of current-period profits. Both firms and the government pay

Table 2 Transaction matrix.

Transaction	Households	Firms (current)	Firms (capital)	Government	Sum
Consumption	$-C(1+\tau)$	$+C$	0	$+C\tau$	0
Investment (gross)	0	$+I$	$-I(1+\tau)$	$+I\tau$	0
R&D Spending	0	$+R$	$-R(1+\tau)$	$+R\tau$	0
Wages	$+wL$	$-wL$	0	0	0
Depreciation of the capital stock		$-\delta K$	δK		0
Interest payments	$+r^B B + r^G B^G$	$-r^B B$	0	$-r^G B^G$	0
Profits	0	$-\text{Profits} = -[(C+I+R) - (wL+\delta K+r^B B)]$	$\text{Profits} = (C+I+R) - (wL+\delta K+r^B B)$	0	0
Subtotal (= cash flow)	$wL + r^B B + r^G B^G - C(1+\tau)$	0	$C - (wL+r^B B) - (I+R)\tau$	$(C+I+R)\tau - r^G B^G$	0
Issuance of Private Bonds	$-\Delta B$		$+\Delta B$	0	0
Issuance of Government Bonds	$-\Delta B^G$	0	0	$+\Delta B^G$	0
Sum	0	0	0	0	0

interest on outstanding bonds to households, which is a source of income for households.[7]

Current-period firm profits are calculated, in the current account of firms, as income from sales minus the sum of wages paid, depreciation and interest paid: $(C + I + R) - (wL + \delta K + r^B B)$. This is added with a negative sign in the current account of firms so that this column will add up to zero. Profits are also entered into the capital account of firms, that is, profits are ultimately added to net worth. The subtotal of the first seven rows (consumption–profits) gives the cash flow of the three types of agents, where the cash flow of firms appears in the capital account of firms (and the subtotal of the current account is zero). The entries in the transaction matrix in this row give the analytical expressions for the cash flow which are obtained by adding the entries in rows 1–7. The cash flows of the three types of agents together sum to zero.

These cash flows are accounted for in the wealth stocks of the three types of agents. A negative cash flow of firms must lead to the issuance of new firm bonds, and similarly, a negative cash flow of the government must lead to the issuance of new government bonds. If the government or firms have a positive cash flow, they buy back bonds that were previously issued. A positive cash flow of households means that they buy bonds, and a negative cash flow means that they sell bonds. These bond transactions are displayed in the two rows of the transactions table that follow the cash flow row.

3.8 Dynamics of the Wage Rate

We follow the earlier version of our model in Meijers et al. (2019) for the specification of the equations that set the wage rate, although we use different parameter values in the simulations that will be documented in what follows. Because the price of the homogenous good is fixed at 1 (as a numeraire), the wage rate is a real wage rate. It is common to all firms, that is, it is a macroeconomic wage rate. Rather than specifying the wage rate directly, we derive it from the variable σ, which represents the share of wages in total income. Because of the identity $\sigma = w/\bar{a}$, and with (average) productivity fixed at the moment that wages are set, the wage rate w is found by multiplying aggregate productivity by σ.

Note that the wage share σ also represents unit wage costs of the homogenous good. With the price of the homogenous good fixed at 1, the quantity $(1 - \sigma)/\sigma$ is the markup over unit wage costs that the firms charge when they sell a unit of the homogenous good (because $\left(1 + (1 - \sigma)/\sigma\right)\sigma = 1$). In other words, if σ

---

[7] We also allow for individual firms holding bonds, which happens if a firm runs positive cash flows for a prolonged period. The transaction table abstracts from this possibility.

rises (falls), the markup that firms are able to charge falls (rises). This markup interpretation is used to formulate the main motivation for the way wage formation works. We assume that when firms are, on average, relatively highly indebted (a high leverage ratio), they are forced to increase their markup (i.e., decrease the wage share σ). On the other hand, when firms are relatively debt-free, we assume that competition can do its work and the markup can fall (σ rises).

This basic idea will be operationalized by assuming a 'neutral' value of the leverage ratio, and an adjustment process of the wage share that potentially leads the leverage ratio to this neutral value. This is illustrated in the graphical representation of the wage share adjustment mechanism in Figure 1. The vertical axis displays a multiplicative factor that is applied to the wage share of the previous period to yield the wage share in the current period. With this factor larger (smaller) than unity, the wage share will rise (fall). The neutral value of the leverage ratio is where the line cuts the horizontal axis, as this yields a multiplicative factor equal to 1. Given the negative slope of the line, the neutral value will become a stable attractor for the leverage ratio: to the right (left) of this point, the wage share falls (rises), and the leverage ratio drops

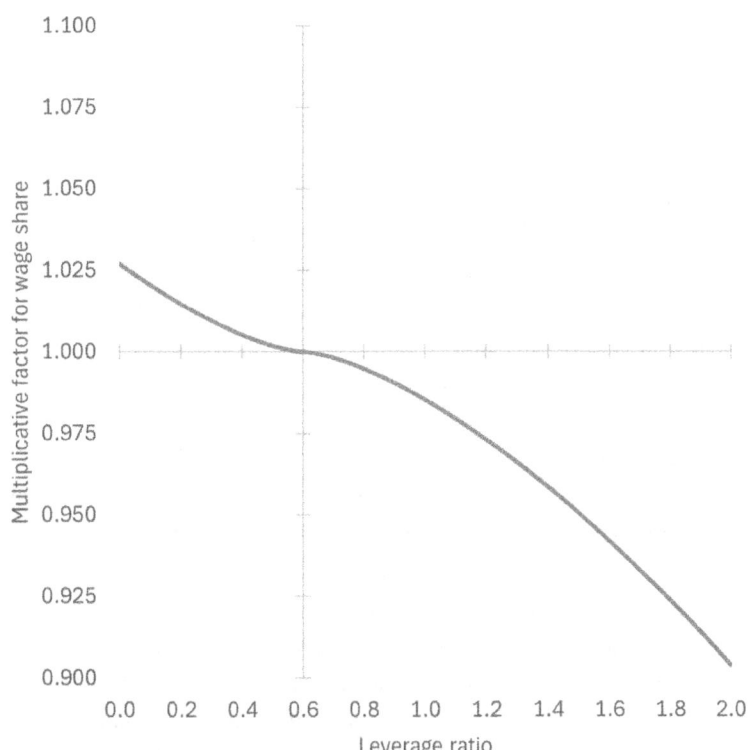

Figure 1 Illustration of the wage share mechanism.

(rises). The non-linear nature of the function implies a short region around the centre where the function is very flat, that is, where the wage share reacts very sluggishly to deviations of the leverage ratio from the centre value. Note also that although the neutral value of the leverage ratio fixes the multiplicative factor at 1, it does not fix the wage share itself. With the multiplicative factor equal to 1, the wage share will remain at whatever it was in the previous period.

For the equations that specify this wage adjustment mechanism, we introduce the new symbol $\Lambda_t \equiv B_t/K_t$ for the leverage ratio. Then, we have the following equation for the (multiplicative) change of σ:

$$\sigma_t = max\left(\sigma^{lo}, min\left(\sigma_{t-1}\Omega_t, \sigma^{hi}\right)\right), \text{with}$$

$$\Omega_t = \begin{cases} min\left(1+\overline{\Omega}, 1+\left(\check{\Omega}|\Lambda_t-\tilde{\Omega}|\right)^{\overline{\overline{\Omega}}}\right) & if \Lambda_t < \tilde{\Omega} \\ max\left(1-\overline{\Omega}, 1-\left(\check{\Omega}|\Lambda_t-\tilde{\Omega}|\right)^{\overline{\overline{\Omega}}}\right) & if \Lambda_t > \tilde{\Omega} \end{cases}.$$

To break this complicated expression down, we first note that the wage share that results from the calculation is bound between a minimum and maximum value, σ^{lo} and σ^{hi}, respectively, that is, if the calculated multiplicative factor Ω_t is either very large or very small, the resulting value for σ_t is capped. The multiplicative factor Ω_t is a non-linear function of the leverage ratio Λ_t, with the parameters $\overline{\Omega}, \check{\Omega}, \tilde{\Omega}$ and $\overline{\overline{\Omega}}$ determining the shape of this function.

The parameter $\tilde{\Omega}$ represents the neutral value for the leverage ratio. Below this centre, the wage share will increase, that is, $\Omega_t > 1$, and above this value, the wage share will decrease ($\Omega_t > 1$). This is arguably the most important aspect of the wage-setting process. At this centre value of the leverage ratio, the wage share does not change (i.e., wages rise proportionately to productivity), while below (above) the centre value, the wage share rises (falls).

Note that in most of the simulations, we set the value of the centre parameter $\tilde{\Omega}$ equal to the value of the leverage ratio at which firms start to become vulnerable to bankruptcy, b^{lo}. There is nothing that dictates that this has to be the case, but we may imagine that $\tilde{\Omega} \gg b^{lo}$ leads to an excessive number of bankruptcies, while $\tilde{\Omega} \ll b^{lo}$ leads to very few bankruptcies. Since bankruptcy is the only form of selection in the model, we must keep $\tilde{\Omega} \approx b^{lo}$ to obtain an interesting selection environment. We will experiment with the difference between $\tilde{\Omega}$ and b^{lo} in simulations that are presented in Section 5.

The other parameters, $\overline{\Omega}, \check{\Omega}$ and $\overline{\overline{\Omega}}$ determine the shape of the wage share multiplication function. $\overline{\Omega}$ limits the line between an upper and a lower threshold. We document this parameter only for completeness; in the simulations that we will report, it is set equal to 1, which implies that in practical terms, there is no threshold. Increasing $\tilde{\Omega}$ will make the function steeper and will rotate it around the centre value in a clockwise direction. Finally, decreasing $\overline{\overline{\Omega}}$ will linearize the function (at $\overline{\overline{\Omega}} = 1$ the function will become a straight line) and also rotate the function anti-clockwise.

3.9 Simulation Results for the Circular Flow: Business Cycles

We will now look at a few basic results from a subset of simulations.[8] The selection of R&D strategies and the productivity changes associated with R&D remain to be specified in the next section. Here we run the model without R&D and productivity growth. Hence the simulation results that we document here have no long-run growth, because there is no technological change. These results are intended to give the reader a basic understanding of the macroeconomic time series that the model in its simplest form generates, and which form the background of our main focus on the disequilibrium state that endogenously determines R&D strategies and the resulting innovation rates in our demand-driven economy.

In presenting those simulations, we focus on the nature of business cycles. This was already a major topic in the predecessor of our model, i.e. Meijers et al. (2019), where business cycles were analysed in the context of the interest rate parameter θ_1 and the wage-setting parameter $\tilde{\Omega}$. However, in our current model, we introduced the consumption-smoothing mechanism that is associated with the household-level variable ζ_j (which was a parameter that applied to all households at all times in Meijers et al., 2019, and a macro-level variable in Nomaler et al., 2021). This changes the nature of the business cycle considerably.

The variable ζ is intended to keep the model on a path without mass unemployment that would result from productivity increase without increased demand. With varying ζ as specified in Section 3.3, the propensity to consume out of wealth, thus autonomous demand will increase if unemployment arises, at least as long as households have enough financial assets to use for consumption. With the household-level adjustment of ζ being non-immediate, and other adjustments (such as investment) also taking place, the time path for the main variables in the model is not expected to be a steady state, and business cycles may arise. In the simulations that follow, we will explore the nature of these adjustment mechanisms in a context without technological change.

Exploration of the model's result (by simulating under a range of parameter values) suggests that the combination of parameter values for α, which represents

---

[8] All simulations in the Element are run using customized code in C# as implemented in Microsoft Visual Studio.

the adjustment speed of ζ in response to deviations of the employment rate from its neutral value, and φ, which measures the responsiveness of investment with regard to deviations of the capacity utilization rate from its neutral value, have a decisive influence on the nature of business cycle fluctuations. In order to illustrate this, we set up a simulation experiment in which we vary both these parameters, with each one taking 11 different values, hence yielding $11 \times 11 = 121$ parameter combinations. For each of those, we run 50 (Monte Carlo) simulations with different random seeds, that is, we run each of the 121 parameter sets with 50 repetitions with different realizations of the random variables; α is varied from 0.005 to 0.025 in steps of 0.002, and φ is varied from 0.025 to 0.055 in steps of 0.003.

In all simulations documented in this Element, we use 50 firms and 150 households, and we simulate for 1,000 periods. All parameter values are as specified in the table in the appendix (Appendix II), but all mechanisms of the model that refer to innovation (which will be specified in the next section) are disabled, so that there is no R&D or labour productivity growth in simulations reported in this section. Figure 2 shows the time series for the last 400 periods of the employment rate in five different individual simulations. These individual runs are arbitrary choices from the 50 random seeds, but we will generalize over the seeds in the next figure. The five time series in the top panel of Figure 2 combine the minimum and maximum values of α with the minimum and maximum values of φ (these are four of the five time series), and one where both parameters are at their middle value. This shows that high values of φ yield high-amplitude cycles. In both cases (high value of φ combined with low and high values of α), the employment rate hits the ceiling that was imposed on labour supply ($\varepsilon = 1.1$), which implies that the economy becomes rationed. In the top panel of Figure 2, this happens only when $\varphi = 0.055$. When we lower these values of φ to 0.049, as in the bottom panel of Figure 2, rationing almost disappears.

The frequency of the observed cycles seems to an important extent determined by α. Looking only at the high values of φ, a higher value of α yields shorter cycles, that is, a higher frequency. This is also the case when we compare α just between the two lowest values of φ. The run with intermediate values of α and φ yields fairly regular cycles with medium-range amplitude and frequency.

This can be generalized by looking at all 50 random seeds for each combination of values of α and φ, which is what Figure 3 presents. For this figure, we performed a Fourier analysis on each individual time series (again for the last 400 periods). We average the outcome of this (i.e., the spectral density) over the 50 seeds, and plot this average on the Z-axis of the sub-graphs in Figure 3. In these 3D sub-graphs, we can only vary one of the parameters α and φ, and we present three plots where α is varied (and φ is kept constant within each plot),

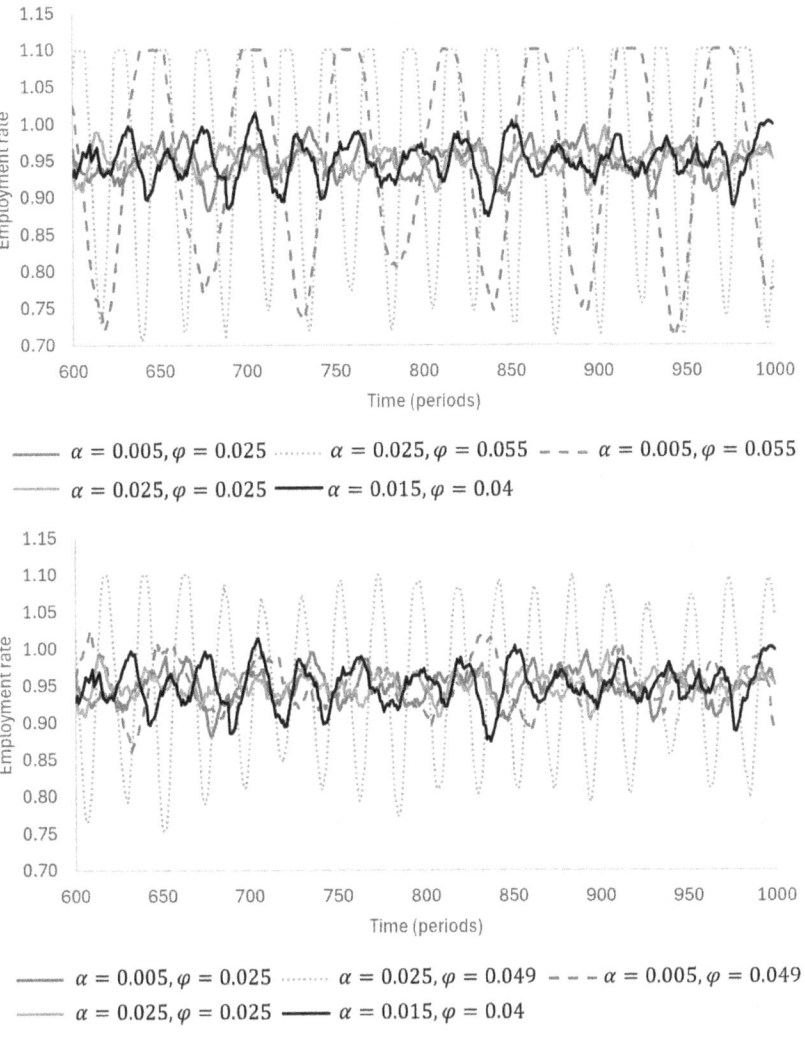

Figure 2 Business cycles showing in the employment rate in individual simulations.

and three plots where φ is varied (and α is kept constant within each plot). Remember that high values of φ (on the φ axis, or in the bottom-left plot) yield cycles where rationing occurs at the peaks of the business cycle.

Figure 3 confirms the impressions about cycle length (periodicity) and amplitude. In the plots where α is fixed (right-hand side) there is very little variation in where the spectral peaks occur on the cycle length axis. In those graphs, we also see that higher values of φ show cycles with higher amplitude, even to the extent that the lower half of the φ range shows almost no cycles, for

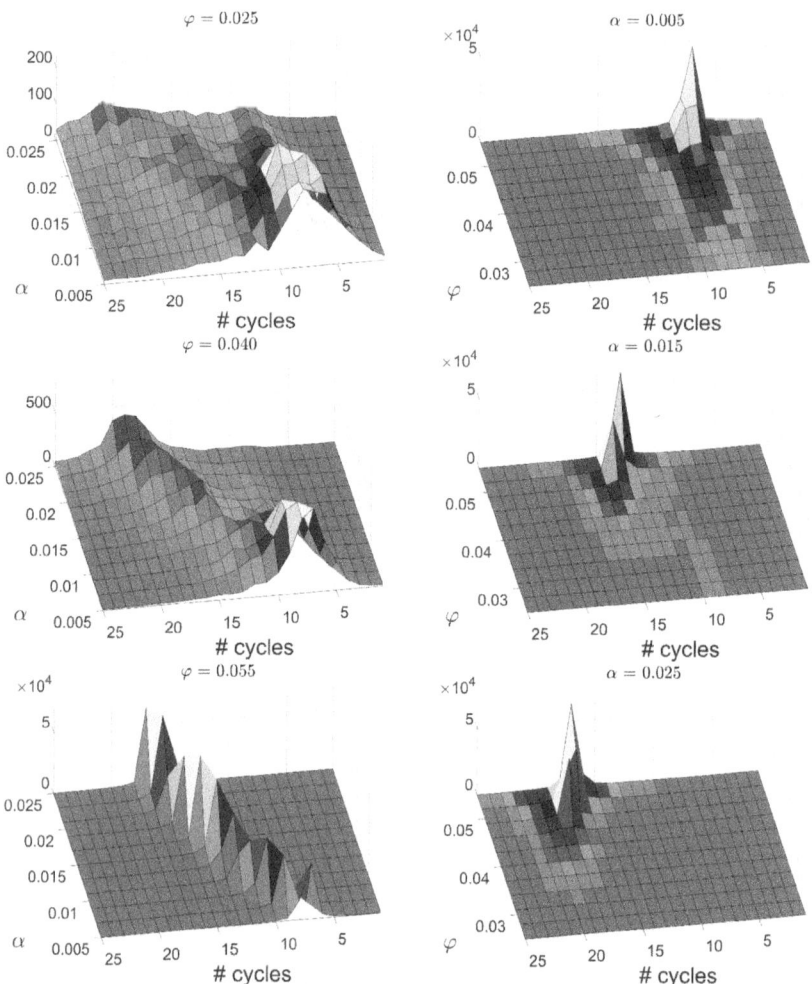

Figure 3 Fourier analysis of the employment rate in individual time series (spectral density on the Z-axis).

any of the values of φ. Thus, to create simulations without (or weak) business cycles, it suffices to pick a value of φ in the range 0.025–0.035.

On the other hand, when we vary α, while keeping φ fixed, periodicity changes in a major way. For low values of α, that is, when consumption smoothing is very slow, we observe long cycles: for the lowest value of α there are about 8 complete cycles over 400 periods, that is, cycles of 50 periods.[9] By increasing α, we see the cycles shortening. For the lowest value of φ (0.025), the long cycle seems to remain alongside a shorter one but for higher values of φ, we only observe about 20 cycles (over 400 periods) for high values of α.

---

[9] Lower values of α (we tried 0.003 and 0.001) yield very long cycles of up to 200 periods.

We conclude this section by looking at time series of individual runs for some other variables than the employment rate. We choose the wage share in GDP (σ), the aggregate share of household wealth spent on consumption (i.e., the average ζ_{jt} as weighted by individual household wealth Z_{jt}^h), and investment as a fraction of output. These time series are documented in Figure 4. We document results for the same values of α and φ as in the bottom panel of Figure 2, thus avoiding the very high values of φ that cause rationing.

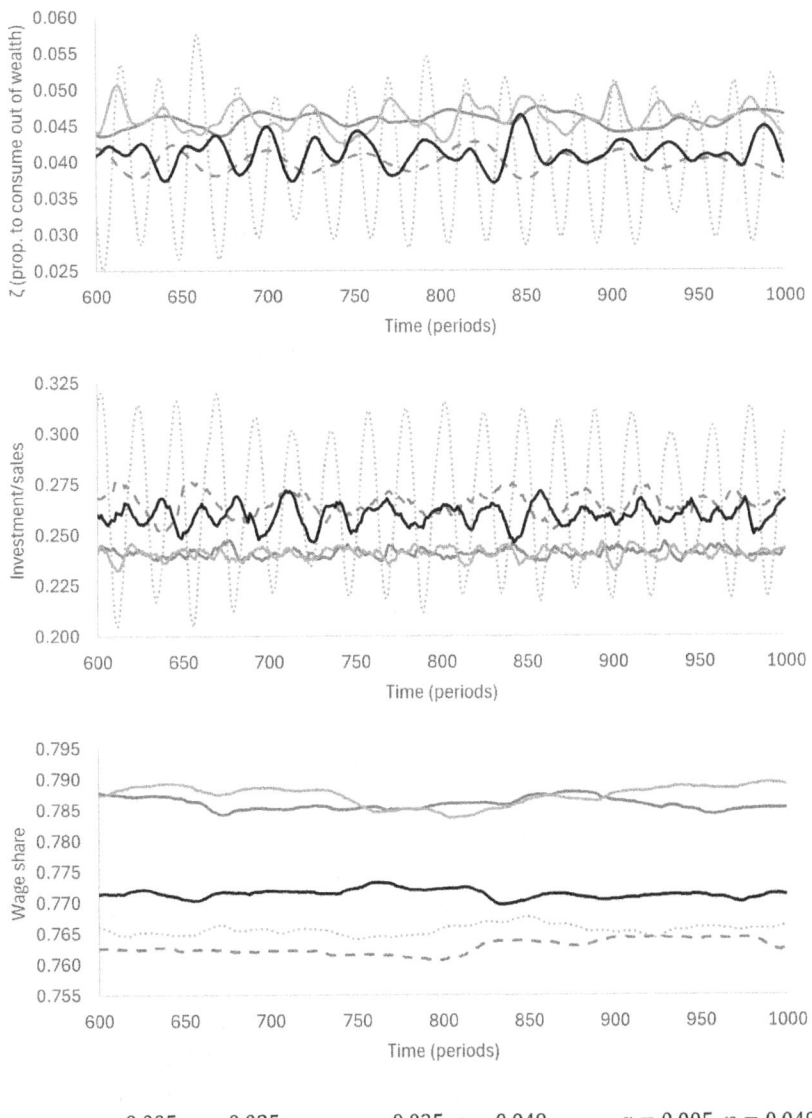

Figure 4 Business cycles for other variables.

In the results for the average ζ and investment, we clearly recognize the business cycle that we saw for the employment rate. Here, we observe long or short cycles, with high or lower amplitude, depending on the values of α and φ. The results for the average ζ show the consumption-smoothing mechanism in action: even for low adjustment speed of ζ in the top panel of Figure 4, the economy never strays too far away from reasonable employment rates in Figure 2.

The wage share is different: we observe a mixture of longer and shorter variations, but these do not clearly correspond to the movements in the corresponding time series for the employment rate. The reason for this is that, given the Ω parameters, especially $\tilde{\Omega}$, the actual leverage ratio of firms (Λ) never deviates very far from its neutral value. This is something that we impose in light of the selection mechanism that we introduce in the next section, and which will ensure that R&D is feasible in our simulated economy.

4 Introducing R&D-Based Productivity Growth

With the Keynesian (demand-side) part of the model in place, it is now time to look at the Schumpeterian part that will specify the dynamics of R&D, innovation and productivity growth. With innovation, the unemployment rate will feel an upward pressure, because labour gets displaced by productivity change. The model as explained so far represents an economy that is able to find a time path with a stationary although fluctuating employment rate, functional income distribution (i.e., the wage share in GDP, σ), and other macroeconomic variables. With the upward pressure on the unemployment rate due to the Schumpeterian process of innovation, achieving a stationary employment path becomes more challenging. This is where the full interaction between Schumpeterian (supply-side) and Keynesian (demand-side) factors comes to play.

In this section, we introduce the aspects of the model that endogenize productivity growth, through the introduction of R&D performed by firms. This is where the agent-based part of the model, in this case the R&D strategies of the firm, is again of central importance. Bankruptcies and the resulting entry of new firms form the selection environment in which firms operate, and in which their R&D strategies are shaped. We will show how the 'stable' macroeconomic environment of the previous section also arises with endogenous R&D, despite the potential of R&D to cause 'technological unemployment', that is, to destroy jobs by productivity increases. This is possible because the adjustment of demand to capacity (through consumption smoothing), combined with the adjustment of wages and σ, will transform increased productivity of firms into increasing living standards for households.

We will explain the process that leads to such a stable macro economy in two steps. First, we look at the cash flow of firms and households. The stability of the leverage ratio that results from the wage-setting process as explained in Section 3.7, has strong implications for other variables through the cash flow equations. In this way, the firms' cash-flow equation specifies a relationship between investment-related variables (the capital-output ratio, the capital utilization rate, and the depreciation rate), the R&D strategies of firms, the resulting growth rate (or productivity), the interest rate and the wage share of GDP. The cash flow of firms is linked to that of households, which brings the (variable) propensity to consume out of household wealth (ζ) also into the picture. The latter variable is a key determinant of autonomous consumption, and, therefore, plays an important role in stabilizing the employment rate.

Although the cash-flow equations, together with a stable leverage ratio, put restrictions on other variables, they do not fix these variables. Importantly, they leave room for variation in the R&D strategies of firms, which, in turn, are an important determinant of growth. Thus, the final step that we will take in this section is the specification of the R&D part of the model. This is where evolutionary selection between firms will endogenize the aggregate R&D strategy. The other variables are determined through the cash-flow equations. All this will be illustrated analytically, as well as by a series of controlled simulation experiments.

4.1 Implications from the Firm Cash-Flow Equation

Imagine that the leverage ratio (Λ) has become fixed at the neutral value $\overline{\Omega}$, and, hence, the wage share is stable between the current and previous periods. What will it take for the leverage ratio to remain at the neutral value and, hence, the wage share to remain stable? The key to this lies in the cash-flow equation of the firm.

Remember that debt of firm B_t is denoted as a positive variable (an indebted firm has a positive value B_t), and that the firm's debt is equal to the sum of negative cash flows from the past. Assuming, for simplicity, that the tax rate is zero, at the aggregate level the negative cash flow is equal to

$$\Delta B_t \equiv B_{t+1} - B_t = Q_{t+1}\sigma_{t+1} + I_{t+1} + \rho Q_t + r_t^B B_t - Q_{t+1},$$

where B_{t+1} is the debt of the firm at the end of period $t+1$, i.e., debt at the beginning of that period (B_t) plus the cash flow that accrues over the period $t+1$ (note that this means we are using a forward difference). In this equation, which holds at the level of the representative individual firm, the first four terms on the right-hand side represent expenditures for the firm: wages associated with the production of goods, investment, R&D (note that current R&D expenditures are the product of the firm's R&D strategy and previous period output, as specified in the previous section) and interest payments, respectively. The final term represents the firm's income from the production of goods. Note that if the firm is not indebted but instead has accumulated a financial surplus in the past, the term $r_t^B B_t$ will be negative and also represent an income.

In the appendix to this section, we analyze the preceding equation for the case of a representative firm. Combined with the cash-flow equation for a representative household and a number of other assumptions, of which the most important one is that there are no bankruptcies, we are able to derive a set of steady-state values for the most important variables in the model. Here we consider the more general case of firm and household heterogeneity, which yields less precise but still interesting conclusions.

The definitions for capacity utilization and the desired capital-output ratio from the previous section imply $Q_t = K_t u_t / v$. We also define the growth rate of output $g_t \equiv (Q_{t+1}/Q_t) - 1$. Then we note that for a stable leverage ratio, the last equation must be set to zero. Doing that and dividing by Q_t, we obtain

$$\rho + r_t^B \Lambda_t \frac{v}{u_t} - \left(1 - \sigma_{t+1} - \frac{I_{t+1}}{Q_{t+1}}\right)(1 + g_t) = 0.$$

This equation enables us to further understand how the leverage ratio can remain stable. As the previous section showed, $\Lambda = \widetilde{\Omega}$ is a prerequisite. Furthermore, we must realize that increasing (decreasing) ρ will generally lead to higher growth (this will be specified more precisely in what follows), and that a higher growth rate of output requires a higher growth rate of capital (i.e., more investment) and/or a higher utilization rate. In other words, there are important dependencies between the variables in the last form of the firms' cash-flow equation. The interest rate r_t^B is the exception to this, as it will be determined in the financial markets.

Imagine, for example, that ρ goes up. This means that the other two terms on the left-hand side of the equation must compensate. Normally, g_t would then also go up, and so would investment as a fraction of output, to accommodate a matching higher growth rate of the capital stock. This leaves the effect on the last term on the left-hand side of the equation uncertain. In the second term, the utilization rate may go up to accommodate the increase in R&D spending. However, the wage share σ may also have to adjust. The equation does not tell us how all these adjustments will balance, but it is clear that changing ρ will have consequences for the other macroeconomic variables.

We can add the aggregate value of ζ to the list of macroeconomic variables that are determined by the dynamics of the cash flow. This variable is an important determinant of the households' cash flow (household income is equal to wage income and interest income, expenditures are consumption spending out of wages and out of wealth). In the appendix, we show that for the representative agent's case, where firm bonds are the only form of wealth held by households, the steady-state value of ζ depends on the steady-state value of σ and the steady-state growth rate. This is likely similar for the more general case with heterogeneity, because government spending plays a modest role in our model, and therefore firm debt is the most important component of the wealth of households.

Households use ζ to regulate autonomous consumption demand so that total consumption is smoothed with varying rates of employment. This process plays the lead role in stabilizing the employment rate, a variable we have not considered so far in this section. The value of ζ that households 'select' will, therefore, play an important role in the overall macroeconomic dynamics of the model.

We will now explore these interdependent macroeconomic dynamics through a number of simulations. Because we will set the value of ρ as a constant between firms and over time within each simulation, these simulations can potentially approximate the representative firm case that is analyzed analytically in the appendix. Depending on how many bankruptcies the specific parameter settings induce, we will be able to approximate the representative firm/household steady state very closely, which provides a clear analytical context for achieving two main results, through simulations of the model as explained so far.

On the one hand, we want to show that the general workings of the model, as explained so far, are compatible with a range of values for the (aggregate) R&D strategies.[10] This is an important point, as it leaves 'headroom' for the selection environment to determine part of the macroeconomic dynamics, that is, to 'pick' a specific set of firm-level R&D strategies that will determine growth and other macroeconomic variables. Without such headroom, there would not be any truly Schumpeterian impact from economic selection. In other words, the ultimate Schumpeterian nature of the endogenization of growth and other macroeconomic variables is, in our model, an evolutionary dynamic process that selects a particular set of outcomes from a wider potentially possible set of

---

[10] This can be formally explained by counting equations and variables. Here we have one (cash-flow) equation with at least five unknowns, while in the case of the representative agents covered in the appendix, we ultimately have two equations with three unknowns.

outcomes. The set of simulation results that will be presented in what follows will illustrate this set of possible outcomes.

On the other hand, we also want to illustrate the trade-offs between R&D and the other main macroeconomic variables that exist in the model, both under the conditions of the representative firm/household steady state (as derived in the appendix), and under more general circumstances of firm and household heterogeneity. In terms of the simulations, this means that we will investigate whether actual simulation outcomes under circumstances that are close to the representative agent case will indeed approximate the outcomes as analytically predicted.

This is the topic of the first set of simulations that we present now: we set parameters in such a way as to yield a situation that is close to the representative agent steady state, as described in the appendix. We use 11 different parameter sets, and for each set, we use 50 random seeds. The fixed R&D strategy that applies to all firms is what varies between the parameter sets. We start with zero R&D strategies (i.e., no R&D) and increase in steps of 0.0075, which makes the R&D strategy in the last step equal to 0.075.

In the simulation experiments in this section, we use a very simple specification of the R&D-to-innovation relationship. Every firm will innovate every period, and each innovation generates an increase in labour productivity of the firm. The size of this increase (the innovation step) depends on the R&D strategy. The relationship between R&D and the innovation step size is an S-shaped function, as in Figure 5. In the next section, we will specify a more elaborate modeling of the R&D–innovation relationship, based on the same S-shaped relationship, but including various elements of stochasticity. For the purpose of this section, such more elaborate modeling only detracts from the purpose of the simulations.

The parameters that we use to create an environment that comes close to the representative agent case are the interest rate on government bonds, r^G, which we set to zero (such that households do not want to hold government bonds and all wealth consists of firm bonds), the interest rate parameter θ_1, which is set to 250, which implies a relatively low interest rate on private bonds ($1/250 = 0.004$, see the appendix), $b^{lo} = 0.7$, which makes firms that have a leverage ratio equal to or close to the neutral value $\tilde{\Omega} = 0.6$ relatively invulnerable to bankruptcy, and parameter $\eta = 0$, which avoids any loss of capital in bankruptcies. All other parameters (except those related to changes of R&D by firms) are as specified in the table of parameter values in the appendix (Appendix II).

In this way, we eliminate all heterogeneities (especially between firms) that we can control. However, due to the stochastic micro shocks to both firms' and

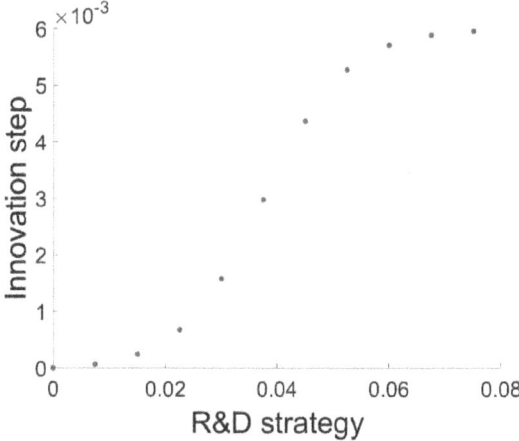

Figure 5 Innovation function used in the simulations.

households' individual cash flows that are inherent to the stochastic workings of the distributed multiplier process that allocates demand (for goods or labour) between agents, substantial heterogeneities in firms' (households') respective debt (wealth) stocks are bound to emerge, especially given the amplifying effect of interest payments (receipts). This path-dependent emergence of heterogeneity introduces a particular kind of noise to our selection environment: some firms are bound to go bankrupt every now and then for no reason other than purely having had bad luck in the (recent) past. This 'emerging heterogeneity' occurs in all simulations throughout the Element.

In this experiment, as in the next one in this section, there is no variability in the growth rates between runs that have the same value for the R&D strategy. This is because the R&D strategies are identical across firms, and innovation is non-stochastic. The growth rates that we observe are equal to the innovation step in Figure 5. In order to save space, we will also not document any results for the employment rate and the capacity utilization rate. These variables converge to 'reasonable' values. The employment rate is always around 0.95. The capacity utilization rate also stabilizes, but sometimes remains above 1. This means that capital has to be worked considerably above the desired rate in some simulation outcomes.

We show results for a set of other variables in Figure 6 in the form of boxplots for the distribution of the results of the simulation runs over the 50 seeds used for each parameter setting. We collect values as the average of the last 100 periods of a single simulation run that lasts 1,000 periods. The red lines within each box denote the median outcome value. The box itself stretches from the 25th percentile to the 75th, while the whiskers identify the most extreme

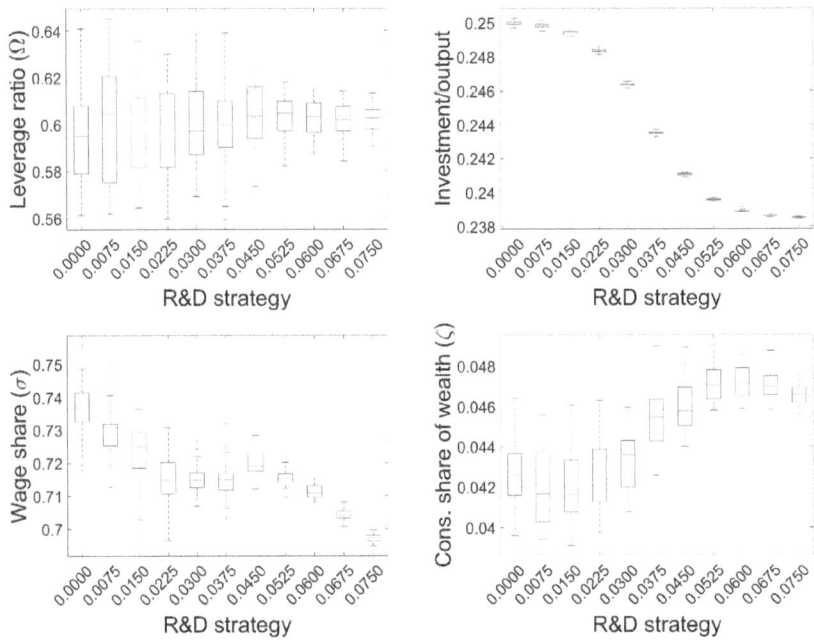

Figure 6 Simulations for approximating steady-state values with varying R&D.

points that still fall within 1.5 times the interquartile range. Any outliers, that is, values that are outside the whiskers, are identified by a +. The horizontal axis of each figure covers the range of values that are used for the R&D strategy that is common to all firms.

In these simulations, for each parameter combination (i.e., an average over 50 seeds), there are never more than 296 (firm) bankruptcies, and never less than 127 (over the full 1,000 periods of a single run). The results for the leverage ratio are displayed in the top-left graph. The distributions (boxes) do not differ very systematically between the values of the R&D strategies, except that higher R&D and hence higher growth) yields a narrower distribution. The median value is always very close to the neutral value of the leverage ratio ($\tilde{\Omega} = 0.6$), indicating that the simulations tend to converge to the steady point of Figure 1. The next graph (top-right) shows the results for the investment-to-output ratio. This declines with higher R&D (and growth rates), as predicted by the derivations in the appendix. This means that the higher capital demand that comes with higher growth rates is partially accommodated by higher capital utilization rates. The next variable (bottom-left) is the wage share σ. This varies over a fairly narrow range of about 5 percentage points. The (median) wage share clearly declines with the R&D strategy, which confirms the expectations from the appendix, although there is a flat part in the middle. Finally, in the bottom right, we have results for ζ, the share of household wealth that is consumed. The median values of this variable tend to rise for the middle range of R&D.

Although there are bankruptcies in these simulations, the values of σ and ζ, as well as of the capacity utilization rate u are relatively close to the theoretical values for the representative agent steady state that we derived in the appendix. We averaged the values obtained for the last 100 periods over the 50 seeds, and compared these averages to the analytical 'steady-state' values that were derived in the appendix. For u, the maximum deviation was about 0.7% (for the R&D strategy equal to 0.075), for σ it was 1.5% (for R&D strategy equal to zero), for investment over output, it was about 0.7% (for R&D strategy equal to 0.075), and the maximum deviation for ζ was about 2.6% (for R&D equal to 0.0075).

We now move to the next simulation experiment, in which we allow for more bankruptcies, and a stronger impact of those bankruptcies, while keeping all other things, including fixed R&D strategies, equal to the first experiment. Now we set $\eta = 0.8$, which implies that 20% of capital is lost if a firm goes bankrupt, and $b^{lo} = 0.6$, which makes a firm that is close to the neutral leverage ratio already vulnerable to bankruptcy. All other parameters are similar to the previous experiment. With these settings, there are considerably more bankruptcies: never less than 727, and never more than 1,004. Hence the outcomes are expected to be further away from the representative agent steady state, which is indeed what we observe.

These results are presented in Figure 7. The leverage ratio is even closer to the neutral value of 0.6. This is obviously due to the different values of the parameter b^{lo} between the two runs. With the lower value in the simulations of Figure 7, it is 'easier' to go bankrupt, but the higher number of bankruptcies also keeps the economy (even) closer to the neutral leverage ratio. The investment-to-output ratio is now lower, the wage share is higher than in the previous experiment (compare the values on the vertical axis), and the intra-run variability (the height of the boxes) is a bit lower. The (downward-sloping) relationship between the wage share and R&D is largely unchanged. Finally, the results for ζ show a discontinuous upward jump at R&D strategy = 0.0525. This is due to a strong rise of debt that is liquidated in bankruptcies, which hurts financial wealth of households, which requires higher ζ for consumption smoothing.

We can draw two major conclusions from these two experiments and the analytical discussion of the equations. First, we must note that the macroeconomic dynamics seem to be able to adjust to various levels of R&D spending, leading to a stable macroeconomic environment, in which some of the crucial

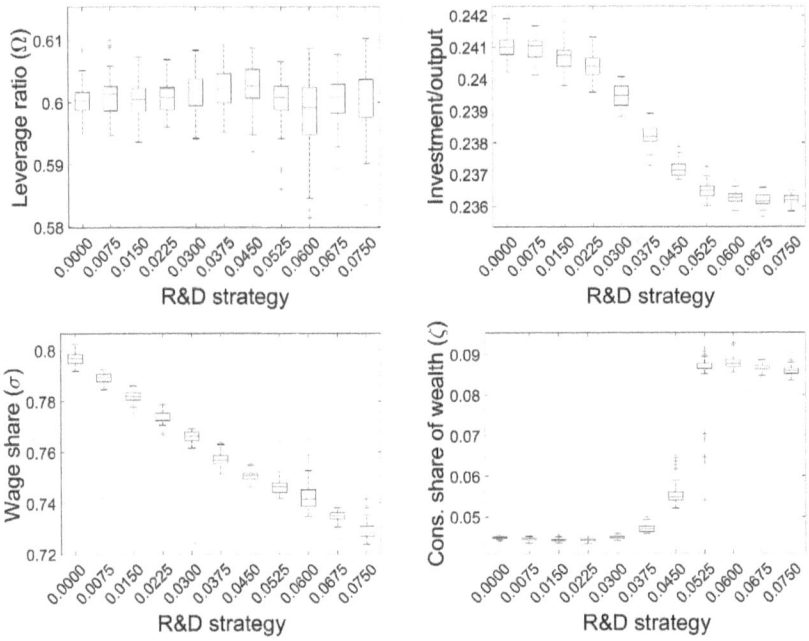

Figure 7 Simulations with varying R&D and more bankruptcies and stronger impact of bankruptcies.

macroeconomic variables change under the influence of R&D. But R&D itself has not yet been endogenized. This means that we still need to build an important part of the model, which 'fixes' the R&D strategies of firms and, therefore, endogenously determines which particular combination of economic growth and other variables, such as the wage share, will emerge. This is the task for the remainder of the section, which will specify how an evolutionary selection mechanism driven by bankruptcies will select R&D strategies.

The second important conclusion is that although our simulation results by and large confirm the analytical expressions for the wage share and the propensity to consume out of wealth that hold in a steady state with a representative firm and representative household, they also show that this can only be done in parameter settings that (largely) eliminate bankruptcies. As soon as we allowed a higher number of bankruptcies, and increased their impact on the macroeconomy, the simulations converged to different values than the steady-state equations of the appendix. Because the evolutionary selection mechanism that we will explain in what follows needs bankruptcies to operate, we must expect that the derivations for the representative agents will be of little value in the analysis of the full model.

4.2 Imitation and the R&D Strategy Parameter

Our main proposal for the endogenization of R&D is that firms will experiment with different R&D strategies in a 'blind' way, that is, they will not choose their R&D strategy based on a rational plan but instead will be randomly endowed with such strategies. Selection in the form of bankruptcies then has the task of weeding out R&D strategies that are not viable in the macroeconomy. As mentioned before, this is not intended as an approximation of the real world. Instead, it is intended to investigate if such a limited and parsimonious evolutionary mechanism is strong enough to allow for a convergence of R&D strategies to a narrow evolutionary stable range (which is resilient against the incessant introduction of mutations of R&D strategies), and what the value of this 'aggregate' R&D strategy implies for the macroeconomic variables, as in the two simulations presented earlier.

The firm is born with an R&D strategy variable that is assigned exogenously (and possibly randomly). There are two ways in which the R&D strategy can change over the lifetime of the firm: whenever the firm goes bankrupt, it will be re-born and imitate the R&D strategy of another firm, or it may change its R&D strategy by random mutation. For the latter, at the closing of each period, the firm draws a raffle ticket that has a fixed probability π^{mut} of bringing a mutation. If the mutation happens, the firm draws a normally distributed random number with mean zero and standard deviation ρ^{up}/B^{mut} and adds this number to its existing R&D strategy parameter. When a negative R&D strategy parameter results, it is set to zero. The parameter ρ^{up} will be explained in what follows, while the parameter B^{mut} specifies a bandwidth for the mutation step.

After bankruptcy, the re-born firm finds another firm that it will imitate. The (re-born) firm that is going to imitate will randomly (with uniform probability) select other firms as potential imitation targets, until it has a pool of n^{imit} targets to choose from (it will select less than n^{imit} targets if it considered all other firms and still found less than n^{imit}). Firms that are about to go bankrupt are not considered as imitation targets, and we also allow for the possibility of very young firms (that have yet to prove their viability in the marketplace) to be disregarded as imitation targets. The latter is implemented by multiplying the uniform probability of a firm to be chosen as target by $min(1, Age_j/\overline{A})$, where Age_j is the age (in time periods) of the potential target j, and $\overline{A}$ is a parameter.[11] Among all potential targets, the one that has the lowest bankruptcy probability is actually imitated.

---

[11] We set $\overline{A} = 1$ in all simulations so that age has no impact on the probability of being an innovation target.

Once the bankrupt-and-reborn firm has found a firm to imitate, adjustments to its debt are made, as described in Section 2. Also, the reborn firm gets a new R&D strategy and a new labour productivity level. For productivity, we have two options, implemented by the parameter *imit*. When *imit* = 0, the new firm receives the labour productivity level of the imitated firm. This usually leads to a fairly large externality because imitated firms tend to be more productive than bankrupt firms. This is why we introduce *imit* = 1, which specifies that the reborn firm gets the economy-wide average labour productivity $\bar{a}_t$.

Independent of the way labour productivity of the reborn firm is determined, its R&D is imitated, although with a (small) mutation. Like in the case of mutation, the reborn firm draws a normally distributed random number with mean zero and standard deviation ρ^{up}/B^{imit}. This is similar to what happens in the case of mutation, but we set $B^{imit} \gg B^{mut}$, so that the random number that is drawn in the case of imitation will usually be much smaller in absolute value than the random number drawn for mutation. The reborn firm adds the randomly drawn number to the R&D strategy parameter of the imitated firm and adopts this as the new R&D strategy.

4.3 Dynamics of Innovation

The only thing that is now left to be described in terms of the model is how R&D affects innovation and productivity growth. For this, we set up two possible ways in which the R&D strategy of a firm leads to innovation and productivity growth. These 'innovation modes' are, in fact, assumed technology landscapes that describe the relationship between R&D expenditures and productivity growth. Although there is work in the evolutionary economics literature that assumes fairly complicated technology landscapes (e.g., NK landscapes, as in Frenken, 2006 and Valente, 2014; percolation landscapes as in Silverberg and Verspagen, 2005), our landscape will be very simple (in line with earlier work in the Schumpeterian tradition, e.g., Silverberg et al, 1988; Silverberg and Verspagen, 1994). This is, again, done to keep the model as simple as possible.

Although, in principle, these two innovation modes could be combined, in the actual practice of our simulations, we do not mix the innovation modes. In mode 1, the probability that a firm innovates depends on its R&D strategy, while the productivity increase that innovation brings is a fixed (i.e., independent of R&D) percentage. In mode 2, the probability that a firm innovates is fixed (independent of R&D), while the percentual productivity increase depends on the R&D strategy. In both cases, we assume for simplicity that only the current period R&D strategy of the firm matters. A firm that jumps from zero R&D in the previous period to some positive R&D strategy has the same innovation probabilities as a firm that has been using the same R&D strategy for a long time.

In the first innovation mode, the innovation step is equal to a fixed size (proportional productivity increase) $\overline{\varphi}^{mod1}$. The probability that a firm j innovates at the end of period t is equal to

$$L_{jt}^{mod1} = \frac{1}{1+e^{-\phi^{mod1}\left(\frac{2\rho_{jt}}{\rho^{up}}-1\right)}}, \quad P_{jt}^{mod1} = \Phi^{mod1}\rho^{up}\frac{L_{jt}^{mod1} - \frac{1}{1+e^{\phi^{mod1}}}}{1 - \frac{1}{1+e^{\phi^{mod1}}}}.$$

The variable L^{mod1} is a (logistic) S-shaped function of the R&D strategy variable. The innovation probability function resembles this logistic curve, but it is re-scaled to yield a maximum probability that is equal to $\Phi^{mod1}\rho^{up}$.

The shape of the innovation probability function for the default parameters is displayed in the top panel of Figure 8. Because $\Phi^{mod1}\rho^{up} = 0.5$ with the default parameters, the function maxes out at 0.5 probability. Note that the parameter ρ^{up} appears twice: it determines both the slope of the logistic function itself and the ceiling of the innovation probability function. Increasing (decreasing) ρ^{up} while adjusting Φ^{mod1} to keep $\Phi^{mod1}\rho^{up}$ constant will stretch the innovation probability function to the right (left), thus making it more (less) difficult to achieve a high innovation probability. The parameter ϕ^{mod1} adjusts the slope of the logistic function independently of the ceiling of the innovation probability function.

In innovation mode 2, we set the probability of innovation to a fixed value $\overline{P}^{mod2}$. Then, the innovation step for firm j is equal to

$$L_{jt}^{mod2} = \frac{1}{1+e^{-\phi^{mod2}\left(\frac{2\rho_{jt}}{\rho^{up}}-1\right)}}, \quad \varphi_{jt}^{mod2} = \widetilde{\varphi}\frac{L_{jt}^{mod2} - \frac{1}{1+e^{\phi^{mod2}}}}{1 - \frac{1}{1+e^{\phi^{mod2}}}}.$$

The shape of this innovation step function is very similar to the innovation probability function of mode 1. The logistic S-shaped function L^{mod2} increases with the R&D strategy parameter. In most cases, when comparing innovation modes 1 and 2, we will set $\phi^{mod1} = \phi^{mod2}$ so that these functions are identical between the modes.[12] The actual innovation step function re-scales the logistic function to reach a maximum at $\widetilde{\varphi}$, which is the maximally attainable innovation step. The shape of the innovation step function at default parameters is displayed in the bottom panel of Figure 8.

One additional aspect of innovation remains to be explained: the influence of firm age. We assume that learning by R&D takes some time after the firm is born

---

[12] Default parameter values for the slope parameters are $\phi^{mod1} = \phi^{mod2} = 2.5$, which implies that at ρ^{up}, the S-shaped innovation function is at about 90% of its saturation level.

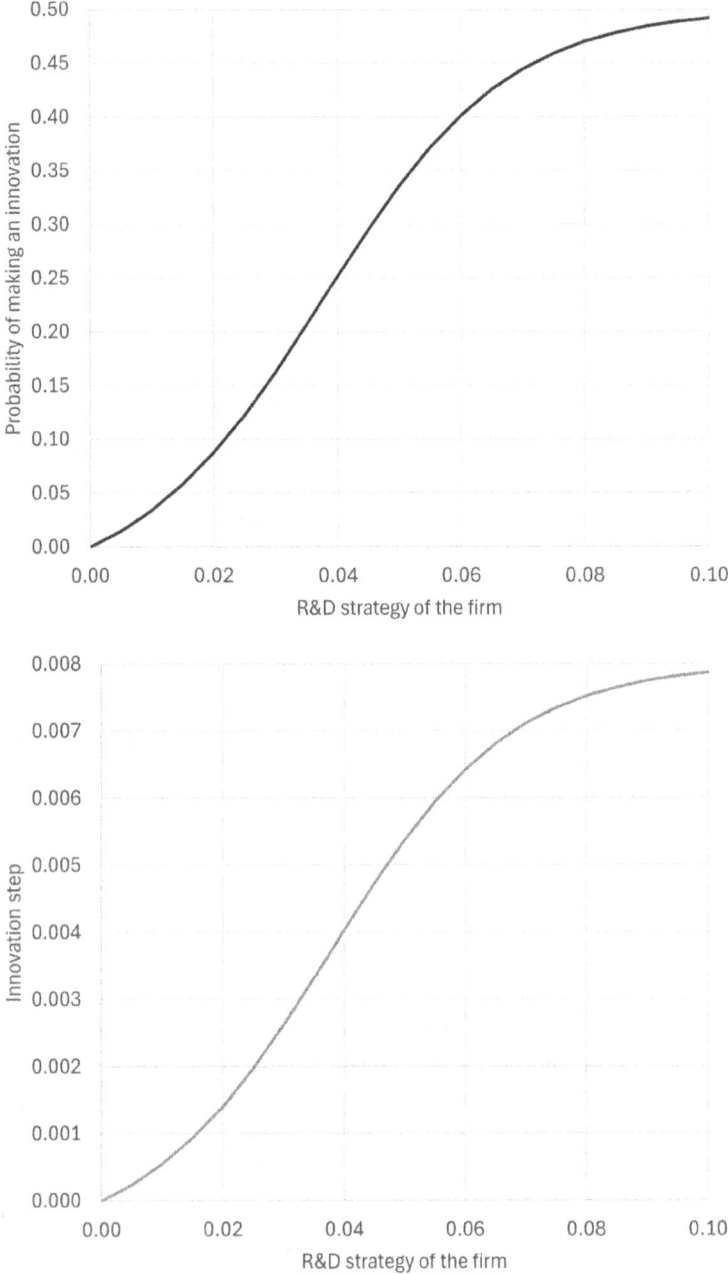

Figure 8 Innovation functions for mode 1 (top) and mode 2 (bottom).

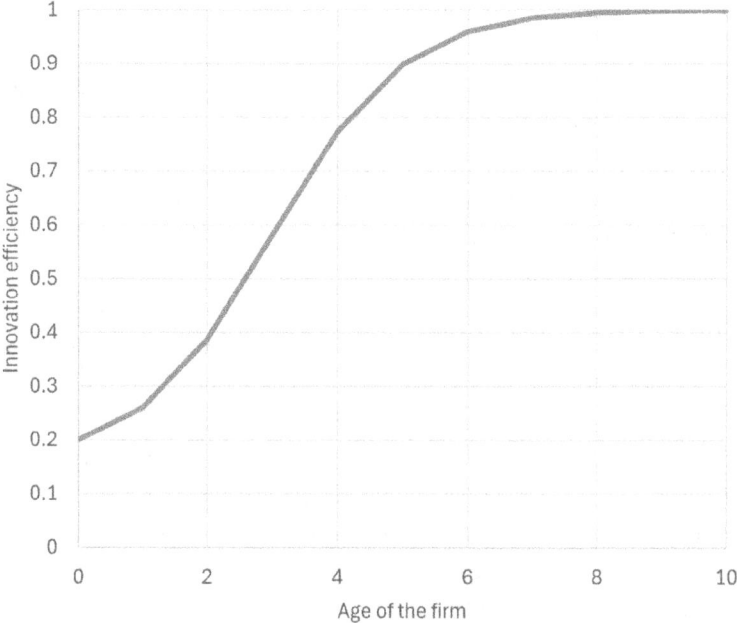

Figure 9 Innovation efficiency function.

out of a bankruptcy, which is in line with the effect of age on the probability to be imitated, as explained in the previous section. In order to reflect this new learning-by-doing effect, we multiply the innovation that a firm realizes by the following S-shaped 'innovation efficiency' function:

$$\iota + (1-\iota)\frac{\frac{1}{1+e^{-(A_i-\tilde{A})}} - \frac{1}{1+e\tilde{A}}}{1 - \frac{1}{1+e\tilde{A}}},$$

where ι is the minimum efficiency, and $\tilde{A}$ is the age at which the function has an inflection point. This function is displayed in Figure 9, using the parameters that are also used in the following simulations.

4.4 Simulation Experiments Illustrating the Selection of R&D Strategies

We are now in a position to run simulations with both the Keynesian and Schumpeterian sides of the model in full operation. This is the first experiment in which the model operates in its full complexity, that is, with R&D free to change under the influence of mutation and imitation. The issue that we will investigate in these simulations is how the selection environment works on diversity of R&D strategies. This is an important experiment, as it will illustrate how Keynesian and Schumpeterian forces interact to endogenously select (or not) an evolutionary stable R&D strategy that leads to growth with a stationary employment path, that is, with endogenous demand matching endogenous productivity growth.

In this simulation experiment, we set the initial R&D strategy of each of the 50 firms to a random value that is uniformly distributed between 0 and ρ^{up}. In the first set of experiments, we have innovation mode 1, that is, R&D influences the probability of an innovation, while the innovation step size is fixed. The innovation parameter settings are as in the appendix table (Appendix II), which imply $\rho^{up} \times \Phi^{mod1} = 0.075 \times 6.667 = 0.5$ is the maximum innovation probability that a firm can reach, and $\overline{\varphi}^{mod1} = 0.006$ or 0.002. We also set $r^G = 0.00075$, the interest rate parameter $\theta_1 = 250$. With these parameter settings, the model will be operating relatively far from the representative agent's steady state, yielding heterogeneity between firms.

Because we want to focus on the heterogeneity between firms within a single simulation, we graph the results of individual runs. All firms start with labour productivity = 1. During the first 50 periods of each run, no innovation takes place, so that the model can adjust from the initial settings. After this, for another 50 periods, firms can innovate (on the basis of their R&D strategies), but no imitation takes place after bankruptcy. In this way, innovating firms can build up a productivity advantage that reflects their R&D strategy (otherwise R&D would not play any role in imitation during the very first few periods after which innovation starts). After 100 periods, innovation and imitation start to operate, and the run continues for another 900 periods. This is how all simulations will operate from now on.

We again illustrate simulation results using boxplots. In this case, the boxplot reflects the distribution of the R&D strategies between firms within a given period. In Figure 10, boxplots are presented for three different simulation experiments, with each experiment occupying one row (i.e., two plots). The boxplots on the left cover the first 120 periods after when innovation and imitation are fully operational (periods 100 – 120 of the simulation), with every fifth period documented in one box. The figure covers the simulation's history from period 220 onwards, but here, only every 30th period is represented in a box.

The first experiment, at the top of the figure, sets the innovation step $\overline{\varphi}^{mod1} = 0.006$, $imit = 1$, so that bankrupt and re-born firms get the average labour productivity of the economy, and $b^{lo} = 0.6$ (firms at the neutral leverage ratio are already vulnerable to bankruptcy). The results of this experiment show what we call an R&D shake-out. Initially, we see a broad distribution that covers the entire range from 0 to ρ^{up}, with the median in the middle, which means that

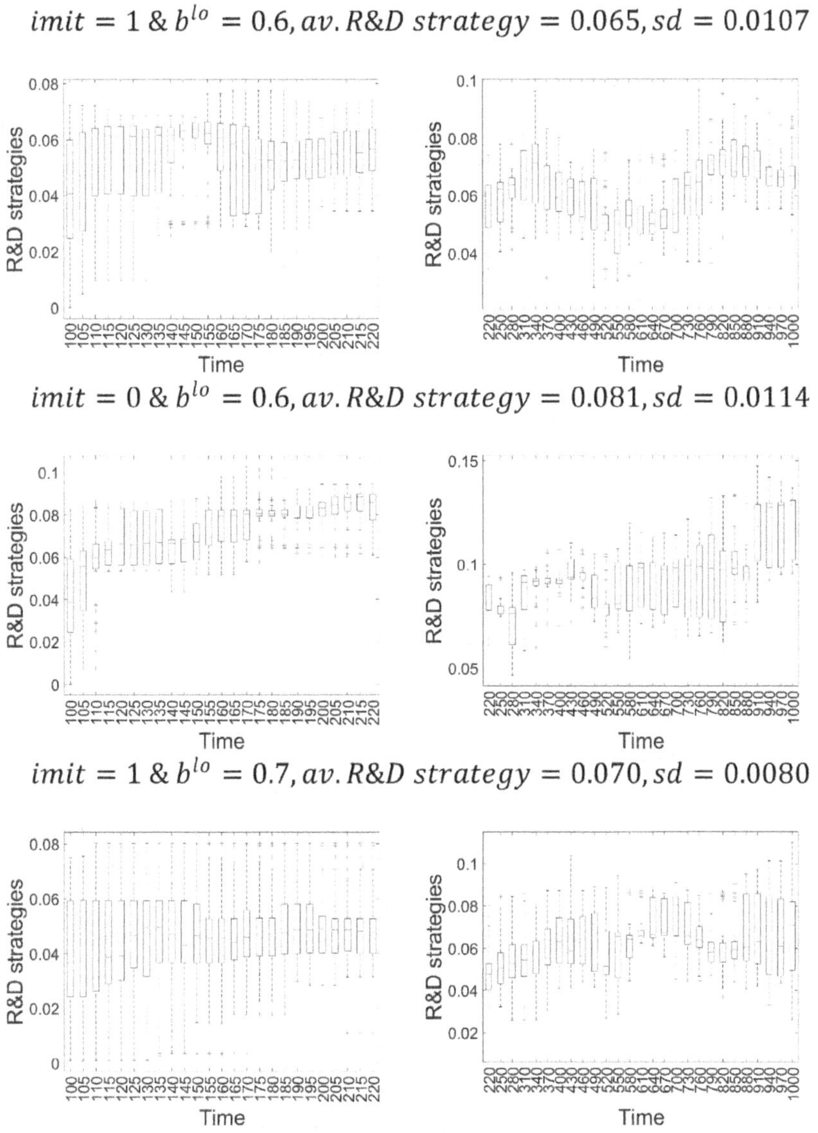

$imit = 1$ & $b^{lo} = 0.6$, $av.\,R\&D\,strategy = 0.065, sd = 0.0107$

$imit = 0$ & $b^{lo} = 0.6$, $av.\,R\&D\,strategy = 0.081, sd = 0.0114$

$imit = 1$ & $b^{lo} = 0.7$, $av.\,R\&D\,strategy = 0.070, sd = 0.0080$

Figure 10 Simulations showing R&D heterogeneity, $\overline{\varphi}^{mod1} = 0.006$.

we are still very close to the random initial distribution. With imitation after bankruptcy kicking in, the median starts to fluctuate, and around period 140, the distribution narrows and becomes skewed towards the higher R&D strategies. Variety in R&D strategies is diminished by selection of strategies in a particular (high) range slightly above 0.06.

The figure on the right-hand side shows boxplots for the remaining 780 periods of the run (note the different scales on the vertical axis). Here the first box (on the left) represents period 220, which is the same period as the end of the graph on the left. We see that the distribution of R&D strategies remains relatively narrow with few exceptions. There is also some fluctuation in the median strategy, but this mostly takes place within the upper part of the zero to ρ^{up} range. This indicates that firms keep experimenting with different R&D strategies, under the influence of mutation as well as small 'errors' in imitation. However, such experimentation is never allowed to move too far away from the R&D strategy that resulted from the shake-out.

Although there are fluctuations of the aggregate R&D strategy, and there is even an intermittent period (460–670) in which lower values prevail, but eventually firms return to values slightly above 0.06. This suggests that firms have converged to an evolutionary stable R&D strategy, and firms that experiment with different (in particular, lower) strategies will eventually not be successful. In other words, the strategy seems to be evolutionary stable. In order to test this further, we repeated this experiment 50 times with different random seeds, and calculated the average R&D strategy over the last 100 periods of each run (this is documented in the figure, along with its standard deviation). Over these 50 random seeds, R&D strategies converge to a narrow range slightly beyond the inflection point as in Figure 8: average 0.065 with standard deviation 0.107.

This is the endogenous selection of R&D that we aimed at in our Keynes–Schumpeter synthesis. As we will explore further in the next section, the outcome of this selection process also determines the other macroeconomic variables, leading to a fully endogenous model with growth and business cycles. In the remainder of this section, we will present a few more simulation outcomes to see whether the emergence of an evolutionary stable R&D strategy also happens with other parameter settings.

The next row in the figure covers a new experiment, with changes in one parameter: *imit* = 0. This is an important aspect of the selection process, as it means that firms that go bankrupt now get the labour productivity level of the imitation target firm at re-birth. This generally represents a very strong positive externality because, with these parameters, imitation targets are about 2% above average productivity in the economy. This externality increases the value of R&D, and it leads to more rapid convergence to a very high R&D value and, up to around $t = 500$, generally, a narrower distribution of R&D strategies.

At the end of this run, we see firms moving up to R&D strategies well above 0.1, which puts them on the ceiling of the innovation function (as in the left-hand side of Figure 8, which reflects parameters of all runs in this section). There is very little 'rationality' to such high values, because R&D has very little marginal pay-off at these levels. We consider this *imit* = 0 as a less interesting (and 'less' evolutionary stable) case and set *imit* = 1 in all simulations in Section 5.

Finally, the bottom row of Figure 10 moves back to *imit* = 1 (no productivity externality), and sets $b^{lo} = 0.7$. Again this changes the selection environment, as it means that selection pressure is lower (vulnerability for bankruptcy starts at a higher leverage ratio). Weaker selection leads to a weaker shake-out: the narrowing of the distribution of R&D strategies takes longer. However, R&D strategies still clearly converge to a high range (in between the values for the other two experiments).

In order to investigate the details of an even wider range of selection environments, these three experiments are repeated in Figure 11, with a much lower value for the innovation step size: $\overline{\varphi}^{mod1} = 0.002$. This means that there are lower technological opportunities, and the pay-off to R&D is generally lower. In the first row, that is, without the productivity externalities (*imit* = 1) and with high selection pressure ($b^{lo} = 0.6$), this leads to a low R&D result. The shake-out eliminates firms with high R&D strategies, because the costs of R&D are too high compared to the pay-off, and the result is an evolutionary stable R&D strategy that is almost equal to zero. In the later stages of the run, there is experimentation with higher R&D strategies (as indicated by the large amount of outliers), but this always fails.

Next, we introduce the R&D externalities (*imit* = 0). This increases the pay-off to adopting higher R&D strategies, and now convergence is to a high level of R&D, as it was with the higher step size in Figure 10. Convergence to the high R&D level is rapid. Experimentation with higher and lower R&D values remains throughout the run, but is largely unsuccessful.

Finally, we have the experiment with lower selection pressure ($b^{lo} = 0.7$), but without externalities (*imit* = 1). In this case, the distribution of strategies narrows, but there are a few firms with higher R&D values that remain alive. This is almost a bimodal distribution, with average and median values in between the two other experiments in Figure 11, but with a relatively high standard deviation. There does not seem to be a clear unique evolutionary stable R&D strategy in this case.

These results do not change in any qualitative way if we use innovation mode 2, where R&D influences the step size and the innovation probability is fixed. We implemented experiments similar to those in Figures 10 and 11 with innovation mode 2 and parameter settings $\phi^{mod1} = 2.5$, $\overline{P}^{mod2} = 0.5$ and $\tilde{\varphi} = 0.006$ or $\tilde{\varphi} = 0.002$. The results resemble those in Figures 10 and 11.

In conclusion, we note that different operationalizations of the selection environment generally lead to very different outcomes of the R&D selection process. When technological opportunities and selection pressure are high

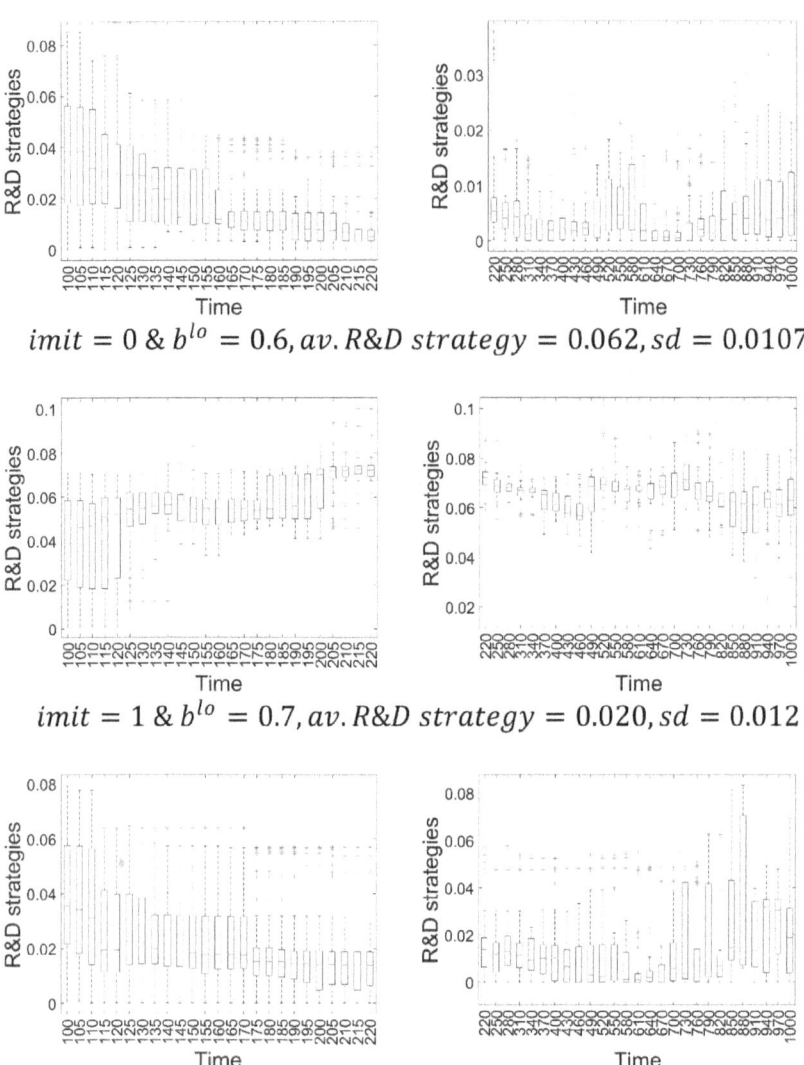

Figure 11 Simulations showing R&D heterogeneity, $\overline{\varphi}^{mod1} = 0.002$.

enough, firms will converge to high R&D strategies that seem to be evolutionary stable. But if selection is weaker (for example, because of financial factors that affect the bankruptcy rate, or because of externalities that give low-R&D performing firms an advantage), R&D may not emerge (or, in other words, the evolutionary stable R&D strategy is close to zero). We will now turn to investigating, in the next section, how these selection dynamics affect macroeconomics, in particular the growth rate and the employment rate.

5 Exploring the Full Model: Monte Carlo Simulations

With the Keynesian and Schumpeterian parts of the model in place, and the R&D selection process shown to be effective, at least under some parameter settings, we are now ready to explore the model more fully by systematic simulations. Despite its relative parsimoniousness, the parameter space of the model is vast. This is why we select a number of experiments that are aimed at various aspects of our theoretical interest, linked both to the Keynesian demand-side and to the Schumpeterian supply-side of the model.

5.1 General Setting of the Simulations

In this section, we will explore the model more completely. Even though the model is kept relatively simple by making only a part fully agent-based, its parameter space is vast. We cannot explore this parameter space in a complete and systematic way. While we carried out many more simulations than what can be documented, we present a selection of what we believe are the most interesting results in light of our main question, which is how the emergence of endogenous R&D can support a growing economy in which demand adjusts to growing productivity while keeping the economy on a more or less stable employment path.

These experiments are organized in the same fashion as the experiment carried out on business cycles in Section 3.6. This means that we will pick two parameters to vary, with 11 values for each of the parameters, and 50 random seeds for each parameter set. This yields a grid of 11×11 parameter sets, each with 50 realizations. We will monitor a set of result variables (e.g., R&D and growth) for each simulation run, and collect average values of these variables over the last 100 periods of each simulation of 1,000 periods. By comparing the distribution of these 50 averages across parameter sets by a t-test, we will investigate how the values of the chosen parameters influence simulation outcomes.

We will present five different 'experiments', that is, five different combinations of two parameters that we vary. In the first of these five experiments, the interest rate parameter θ_1 is one of the parameters that are varied, and we pick different second parameters for each of the four experiments. In the final experiment, θ_1 will be fixed.

The first experiment is aimed at investigating the emergence of a (more or less) stable R&D strategy across the population, from an initial state in which all firms have equal R&D strategies, including the case where no firm carries out any R&D. In other words, this is a generalization of the earlier experiments in Section 4.4, where we documented the microdynamics of the evolution of R&D strategies.

In the second experiment, we explore the difference between innovation mode 1 and mode 2. Here we will specify a parameter set where a firm that spends the maximum amount of R&D, that is, a firm that reaches the ceiling of the innovation curves in Figure 8, has an equal expected productivity increase between the two modes. In mode 1, this is achieved by maximizing the innovation probability with a given step size. In mode 2, the innovation probability is given, and the step size is maximized by doing R&D. We ensure that the multiplication of step size and probability remains constant for a firm at the ceiling of the innovation curve.

In the third experiment, we will look at some of the parameters that affect the financial situation of firms, again generalizing some of the experiments from Section 4. This includes the value of the neutral leverage ratio, $\widetilde{\Omega}$ and the minimum level of the firm's leverage ratio at which the firm becomes vulnerable to bankruptcy, b^{lo}. We vary these parameters simultaneously, keeping them at a fixed distance from each other throughout the experiment.

In the fourth experiment, we look at the interaction between R&D and consumption. Here we vary the marginal propensity to consume out of wage income (c), and investigate whether this influences the R&D strategy that firms converge to. This experiment illustrates how demand and supply interact in our model, through the channel of the firms' cash-flow equation.

Finally, in the fifth experiment, we return to the topic of business cycles. Here we run experiments similar to the business cycle experiment of Section 3, but with endogenous R&D, and investigate the nature of business cycles using Fourier analysis.

5.2 Emergence of R&D

Our first set of experiments is aimed at further exploring the nature of the selection process that determines whether R&D emerges at all. This is a generalization of the experiments in the previous section. In this set of experiments, the main 'parameter' that is varied is the initial level of the R&D strategy. This is specified as a fraction of $\rho^{up} = 0.075$, for example, initial R&D = 0.5 means that all firms start with R&D strategy 0.0375. We vary initial R&D from 0 (no R&D initially) to 1 in steps of 0.1, that is, 11 values. The issue that we want to investigate is whether the level of R&D that emerges at the end of a simulation run varies systematically by its starting value.

As mentioned earlier, the other parameter that is varied is the interest rate parameter θ_1, which ranges from 100 to 400. Note that the interest rate spread between the public and private rates tends to $1/\theta_1$ (see the appendix Section 4.5). Hence, we increase θ_1 in a nonlinear way, such that $1/\theta_1$ decreases in fixed steps of 0.00075. For example, starting with $\theta_1 = 100$, the spread $1/\theta_1 = 0.01$, and, in the next step, we set $1/\theta_1 = 0.00925$, so that $\theta_1 \approx 108.108$, up until at the last step $1/\theta_1 = 0.0025$, or $\theta_1 = 400$.

Figure 12 shows the main modality in presenting the outcomes of a simulation experiment. On the left-hand side, we present 3D surface diagrams for four main outcome variables: aggregate R&D strategy (R&D as a fraction of output), the growth rate (of labour productivity), the wage share σ and the fraction of household wealth spent on consumption ζ. Each of the points in these surface diagrams represents one parameter setting (a combination of θ_1 and initial R&D), and the value on the Z-axis is obtained by first averaging the value over the last 100 periods of a 1,000-simulation run, then averaging those averages over the 50 random seeds that are used for each parameter set.

The diagrams on the right-hand side provide an indication of the statistical significance of differences within each of the surface diagrams. These 'significance maps' belong to the surface diagram on their left-hand side. Each cell in the significance map corresponds to one parameter set, that is, the significance maps can be imagined as the 'floor' of the box in which the surface diagrams are plotted (but note that the floor in the actual surface diagram is rotated). The significance maps are based on the *p*-values of a *t*-test (assuming unequal variances) for the null hypothesis that the average (over 50 seeds) of a value in the surface diagram is equal to the centre cell of the surface diagram. In the case of this experiment, the centre cell of the surface diagram corresponds to initial R&D = 0.5 and $1/\theta_1 = 0.00625$. Thus, for example, the bottom-left cell of the significance map represents the *t*-test for the null hypothesis that the outcome for R&D = 0.0 and $1/\theta_1 = 0.0025$ is equal to that of R&D = 0.5 and $1/\theta_1 = 0.00625$. Statistical significance of these tests is indicated according to the coding in Figure 13. By definition, the centre value is always white.

This experiment consists of three sub-experiments: we run each of the 121 initial R&D and θ_1 combinations in innovation mode 1, for three different values of the (fixed) innovation step size $\overline{\varphi}^{mod1}$. The values for $\overline{\varphi}^{mod1}$ are 0.006, 0.004 and 0.002, corresponding to high, medium and low technological opportunities. All other parameter values are as in the appendix (Appendix II), thus $\Phi^{mod1} = 6.667$, which implies that the maximum innovation probability in a given period is 0.5 (this is obtained by spending enough on R&D).

Figure 12 shows the simulation results for the setting with high technological opportunities ($\overline{\varphi}^{mod1} = 0.006$). For R&D, we see that the average value of the R&D strategy reached at the end of the simulation is higher for cases where the initial R&D is higher, and also for cases where the interest spread is lower. This is clear from the curvature of the surface diagram for R&D, and also from the corresponding significance map: compared to the centre cell, runs with low

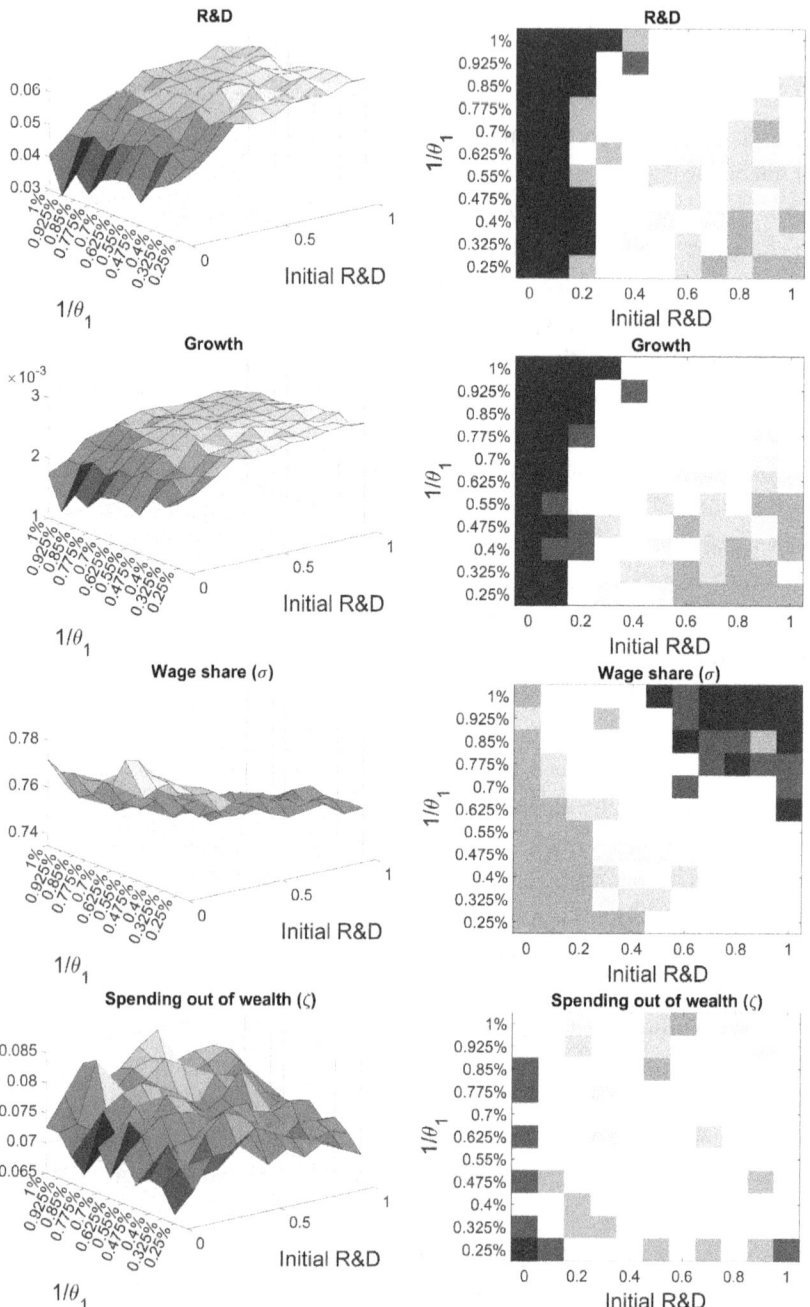

Figure 12 Varying initial R&D against the interest rate parameter θ_1, $\overline{\varphi}^{mod1} = 0.006$.

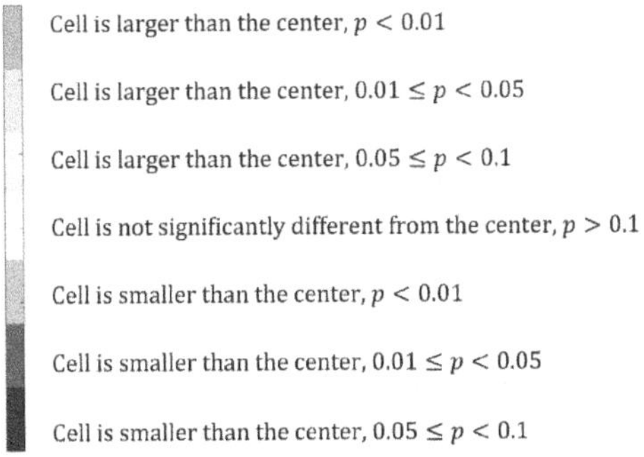

Cell is larger than the center, $p < 0.01$

Cell is larger than the center, $0.01 \leq p < 0.05$

Cell is larger than the center, $0.05 \leq p < 0.1$

Cell is not significantly different from the center, $p > 0.1$

Cell is smaller than the center, $p < 0.01$

Cell is smaller than the center, $0.01 \leq p < 0.05$

Cell is smaller than the center, $0.05 \leq p < 0.1$

Figure 13 Legend for significance maps

initial R&D show significantly lower R&D averages at the end, and those with initial R&D tend to score higher, except for high interest rate spreads.

The lowest R&D value observed in the grid of 121 parameters sets is about 0.03, and it is observed at initial R&D = 0. This means that although all firms started at zero R&D, they converged to at least 3% at the end, and in almost all cases significantly more than 3%. In some cases, they converged close to 7%. This happens only for values of initial R&D close to 1, that is, in those cases R&D stayed very close to what it was at the beginning of the run. All this suggests that in this environment of high technological opportunities, moderately high R&D spending is what firms converge to, but it may take a significant amount of time to get to high levels of R&D spending if firms start at low levels.

Results for growth rates follow R&D closely, as can be expected because R&D translates into higher productivity growth. Still, the significance map for growth is slightly different from that of R&D, due to stochastic variations. The wage share and spending out of household wealth also show significant variation over the parameter sets. Low R&D spending and low interest rates lead to a higher wage share. This can be understood from the firm's cash-flow equation: the more it spends on R&D, the less it can afford to spend on other cost items, such as wages. Thus, when the selection environment presses for more R&D, and firms are not allowed to become more indebted because the neutral leverage ratio does not change, wages must fall. The same mechanism works for interest rates: a high spread leads to higher interest payments and lower wages (as well as lower R&D).

Finally, the results for ζ show less variation than the other variables: the significance map is largely white in this case. Only the edges of the simulation grid show significant variation. With low initial R&D, households spend less of their wealth, presumably because there is less need to compensate for falling employment due to rapid productivity growth. On the other hand, when interest rates are high, consumers tend to spend a larger fraction of their wealth, which is a faint reflection of the steady expressions for this variable.

Next, Figure 14 looks at the case of intermediate technological opportunities. In this case, the runs that start at zero initial R&D hardly escape this low level: they end at around 1% R&D. However, at initial R&D levels around 0.4, a fairly high level of R&D is reached at the end of the simulations. Overall, firms reach lower levels of R&D spending than in the previous case of high technological opportunities. This suggests that in this case, there is a lock-in to low R&D strategies because firms that 'try to' escape from very low R&D level do not survive long enough to reap the benefits of doing more R&D. However, when all firms start collectively with higher R&D levels, this high level can be sustained. These differences are clearly visible in the significance map, which leaves less white and has much more blue than in the case of Figure 12. Results for growth are fully in line with those of R&D.

For the wage share, the general shape of the surface diagram and the significance map look similar to that in Figure 12, although there is an area with intermediate interest rate spread and low R&D that does not differ significantly from the centre. Results for ζ show more differences within the experiment than before. This is mostly due to low values of ζ in the range where R&D locks into a low level.

Finally, Figure 15 shows results for the simulations with low technological opportunities. Here we see that although there are small variations depending on initial R&D, there is never any real take-off of R&D. Aggregate R&D spending never comes above 0.2%. In this case, runs with initial R&D close to or equal to 1 still have higher R&D, which suggests that these runs take a long time to come down to the low levels of R&D that seem to be the attractor in this regime of technological opportunities. Performing R&D does not yield enough advantages to compensate for the costs. Growth is correspondingly low. There are, however, still significant variations in the wage share as well as in ζ, but these seem to depend more on the interest rate spread than on initial R&D (especially variations in ζ).

The conclusion from these experiments is that emergence of R&D crucially depends on technological opportunities and also takes time, especially when technological opportunities are low. Even without rationality at the firm level, that is, with evolutionary selection alone, the population of firms 'discovers' that R&D does not always pay off, which moderates the growth potential (and realization) of the economy.

Keynes–Schumpeter Macroeconomics 59

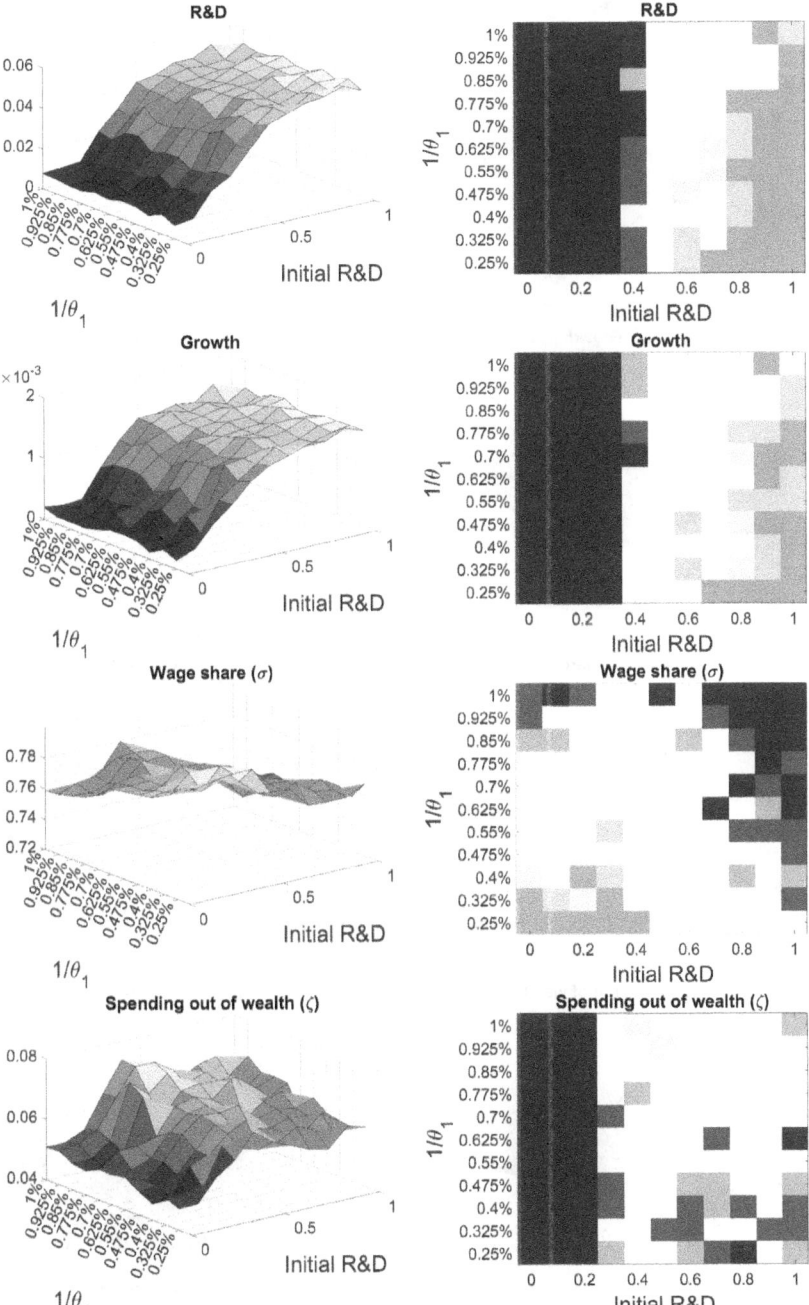

Figure 14 Varying initial R&D against the interest rate parameter θ_1, $\overline{\varphi}^{mod1} = 0.004$.

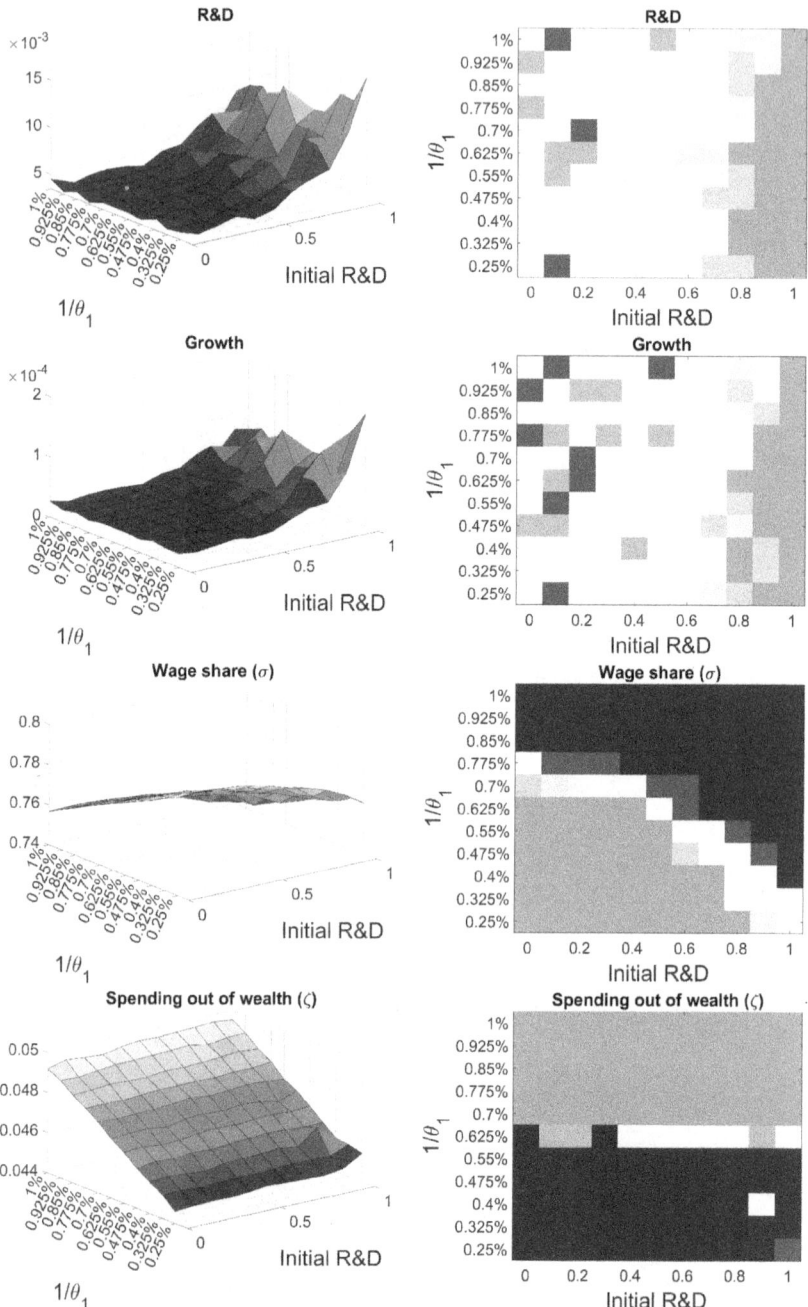

Figure 15 Varying initial R&D against the interest rate parameter θ_1, $\overline{\varphi}^{mod1} = 0.002$.

5.3 Innovation Waiting Time

In the next pair of experiments, we continue the investigation of the innovation process by focusing on the exact way in which innovation influences productivity growth. Specifically, we investigate whether any differences arise between innovation mode 1 and innovation mode 2. For this, we start with an experiment using innovation mode 2. Besides θ_1, which is varied as in the previous section, we now vary the parameter $\overline{P}^{mod2}$, which represents the exogenous probability that a firm innovates. $\overline{P}^{mod2}$ is varied from 0.1 to 1, in steps of 0.09, and the middle value for $\overline{P}^{mod2}$, used in the construction of the significance maps, is 0.55. If the innovation is realized, the innovation step size depends on the R&D strategy, as explained in Section 4.3. In this experiment, the maximum step size that can be obtained, denoted by $\widetilde{\varphi}$, is varied together with $\overline{P}^{mod2}$, in such a way that $\widetilde{\varphi} \times \overline{P}^{mod2} = 0.002 \rightarrow \widetilde{\varphi} = 0.002/\overline{P}^{mod2}$, that is, the maximum step size falls when the innovation probability increases. All other parameter values are as in the appendix table (Appendix II). Each firm starts with R&D strategy equal to 0.0375.

Note that $\widetilde{\varphi} \times \overline{P}^{mod2}$ is the expected innovation step in each period for the firm that spends enough on R&D to reach (close to) the ceiling of the innovation curve as displayed in Figure 8. This expected innovation step remains constant in the entire experiment, but when we vary $\overline{P}^{mod2}$ and $\widetilde{\varphi}$, the expected waiting time for an innovation changes. Obviously, with $\overline{P}^{mod2} = 1$, there is no waiting time, as the firm innovates every period, while with $\overline{P}^{mod2} = 0.1$, the firm will have to wait, on average, 10 periods between innovations. R&D expenditures during this waiting time will represent costs, and hence increase the debt burden of the firm, while no productivity increase is forthcoming during such waiting time.

Note also that these simple calculations of the expected innovation for each period do not take into account compounding of productivity. In a simulation where firms innovate often, that is, where $\overline{P}^{mod2}$ is large, compounding provides an advantage over runs where $\overline{P}^{mod2}$ is lower. For example, with $\overline{P}^{mod2} = 1$, a firm that manages to get the maximum step size $\widetilde{\varphi}$ all the time will have increased productivity by $(1 + \widetilde{\varphi})^{10}$ after 10 periods, while in the case of $\overline{P}^{mod2} = 0.1$, a firm that has to wait until period 10 for an innovation will have a productivity increase of $(1 + 10\widetilde{\varphi})$, which is smaller than $(1 + \widetilde{\varphi})^{10}$. Thus, in principle, larger $\overline{P}^{mod2}$ should give firms an advantage. However, in our setup, all firms in a single simulation have the same value for $\overline{P}^{mod2}$, so that there is no direct competition between large and small values of $\overline{P}^{mod2}$. We can only compare aggregate outcomes for different values of $\overline{P}^{mod2}$.

In the first instance, this innovation mode 2 experiment is aimed at investigating whether this variation in waiting time and the corresponding

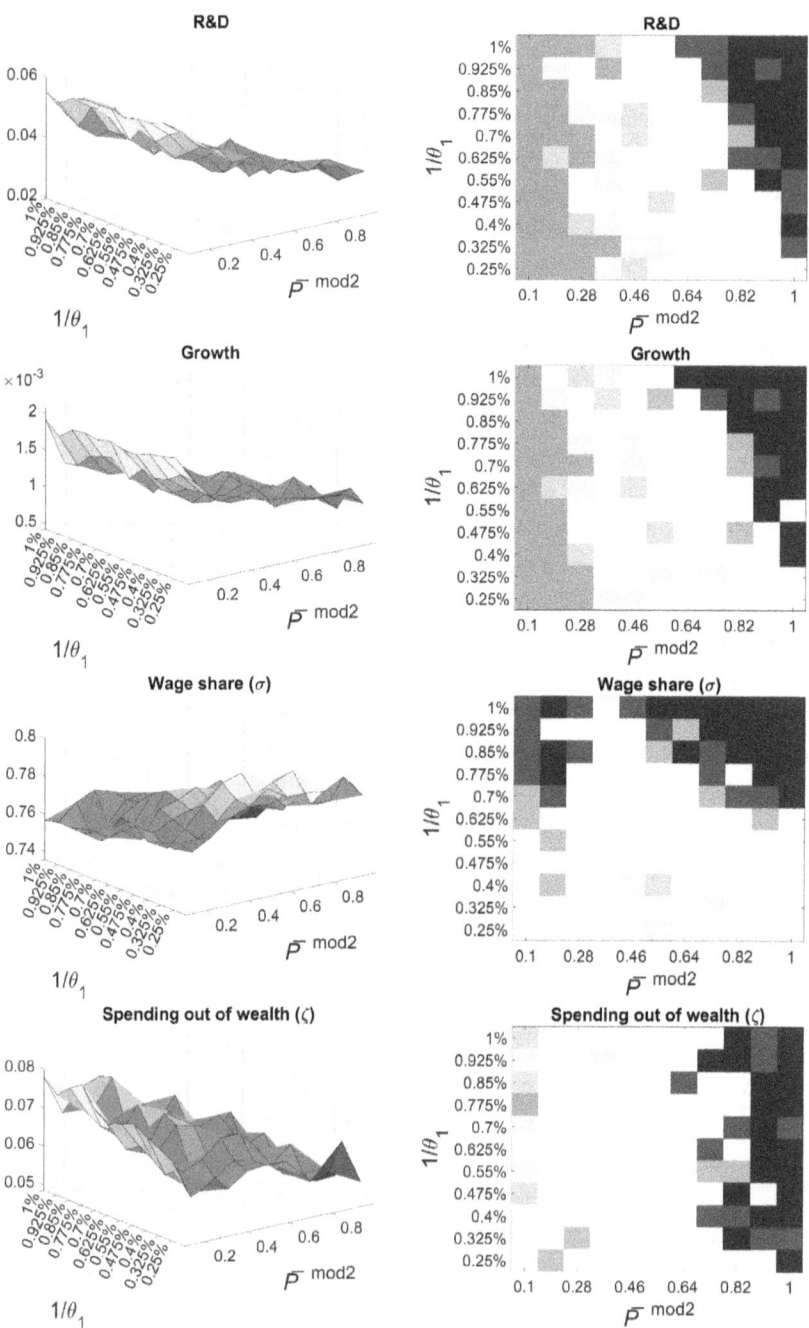

Figure 16 Varying the exogenous innovation probability $\overline{P}^{mod2}$ (mode 2) against the interest rate parameter.

increased step size have an impact on R&D spending. This experiment is documented in Figure 16, which has similar information as in the figures in the previous section. In the two top rows, we see a clear impact of varying the waiting time and innovation step size on R&D levels and growth at the end of the simulations. Interestingly, a long waiting time (i.e., $\overline{P}^{mod2} = 0.1$) combined with a larger innovation step size yields higher R&D spending than a short waiting time with a low step size. This effect is stronger for high interest rates. It is not easy to trace the 'evolutionary logic' of this result with certainty. When $\overline{P}^{mod2}$ is low, firms will, on average, have to survive longer periods without increasing productivity. Higher R&D spending will yield a higher productivity buffer that can be used to outlive these periods, but it also raises costs, thereby indebting the firm more. In this particular setting, the productivity buffer effect seems to outweigh the R&D debt effect. But this may change in other parameter settings, such as a different slope (ϕ^{mod2}) of the innovation function in Figure 8. We leave simulations to explore this further to future work.

In this experiment, the wage share seems mostly influenced by the interest rate spread, although there is a range in the graph for intermediate-low $\overline{P}^{mod2}$ and high interest rates spread where the wage share is relatively high. Spending out of wealth (ζ) mostly varies proportionally with $\overline{P}^{mod2}$.

Next, an equivalent of this experiment is run with innovation mode 1. In this case, the innovation step size ($\overline{\varphi}^{mod1}$) is fixed for all firms throughout a single simulation run, but the 'R&D efficiency' parameter Φ^{mod1} is adjusted. Note that $\Phi^{mod1} \times \rho^{up}$ defines the maximum innovation probability in mode 1. ρ^{up} remains fixed at 0.075, so that the maximum expected innovation step that a firm can have is $\Phi^{mod1} \times 0.075 \times \overline{\varphi}^{mod1}$. While we change Φ^{mod1}, we simultaneously vary $\overline{\varphi}^{mod1}$, in such a way that $\Phi^{mod1} \times 0.075 \times \overline{\varphi}^{mod1} = 0.002$, which is the same value as in the previous experiment. All other parameter values than those relating to the innovation mode are the same as in the experiment of Figure 16.

These results are displayed in Figure 17. At first sight, the results are similar to those in Figure 16. R&D and growth similarly fall with the maximum attainable innovation probability, the wage share remains mostly influenced by the interest rate spread, and consumption spending out of wealth by R&D. However, the significance maps show a weaker effect, that is, there is more white in those maps in Figure 17 than in Figure 16.

Figure 18 shows the significance maps for the t-tests that compare the means of the corresponding cells from the mode 2 experiment (Figure 16) and the mode 1 experiment (Figure 17). This always compares one cell in the 11×11 grid of parameter sets to the same cell in the other experiment. A negative

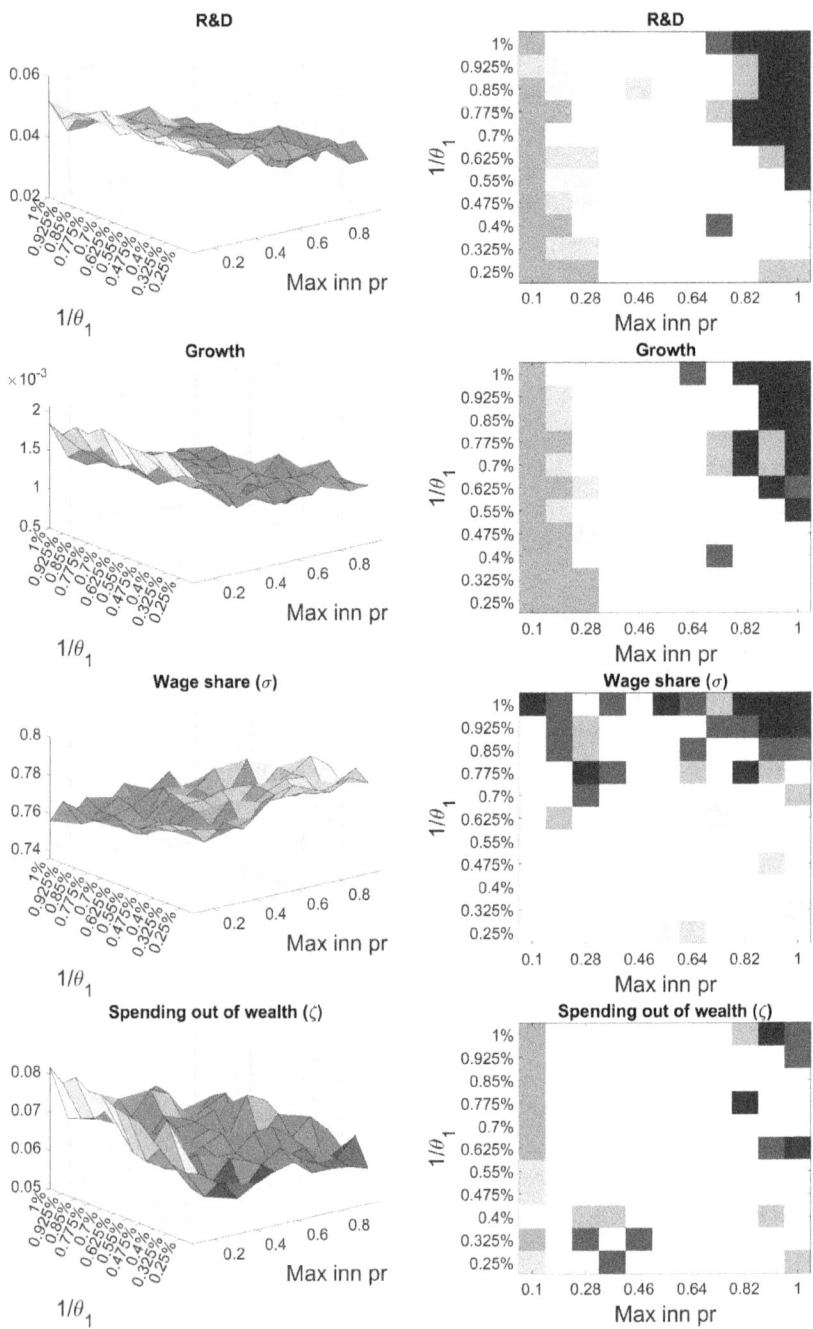

Figure 17 Varying the maximum attainable innovation probability (mode 1) against the interest rate parameter.

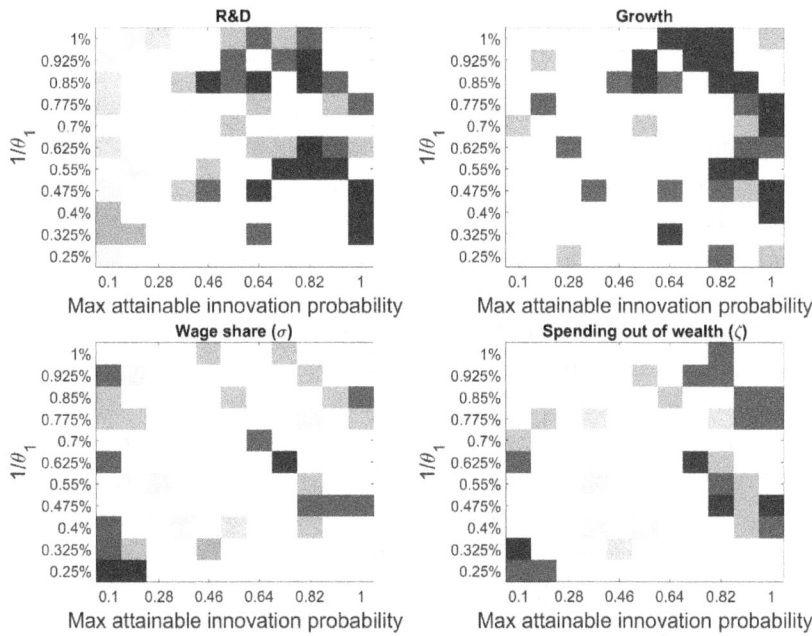

Figure 18 Comparing the two waiting time experiments: significance maps for results of mode 2 simulations minus those of mode 1 experiments.

(positive) sign in these tests indicates that the value in the mode 2 experiment was smaller (larger) than in the mode 1 experiment.

Despite the fact that the outcomes of the two experiments look similar, there are clear and significant differences between the two innovation modes. For example, the mode 2 experiment almost always results in significantly higher R&D when the (maximum) probability of innovation is close to 0.1, that is, the left side of the significance maps. At the same time, it results in lower R&D in the diagonal band in the significance maps near the right-upper corner, that is, with high interest rate spreads and low (maximum) probability of innovation. However, these differences do not translate so clearly into similar differences in growth, probably because of stochasticity, especially in terms of high-productivity firms going bankrupt. Overall, mode 2 seems to result more often in lower values of all the variables than in higher values.

The conclusion from these experiments is that the nature of the R&D and innovation processes also influences growth. Whether innovation tends to take place in small or large steps, and how this can be influenced by the R&D that the firm undertakes leads to different growth outcomes. Of course, in reality, there are many more aspects of innovation that can be influenced by R&D, and hence, we may expect an even larger variety in growth.

5.4 Finance and Selection: Varying the Neutral Leverage Ratio and Minimum Bankruptcy Vulnerability

As the final experiment on the Schumpeterian (innovation) side of the model, we continue the analysis of the selection environment. However, instead of looking at the nature of R&D and innovation, we now explore the impact of financial factors as they influence the bankruptcy of firms. We continue with the familiar setup of the experiments, that is, varying parameters in two dimensions in an 11×11 grid. As before, one of the dimensions of this grid is the interest rate parameter θ_1. In the other dimension of the grid, we vary two parameters at the same time: the neutral leverage ratio $\widetilde{\Omega}$ and the minimum bankruptcy vulnerability b^{lo}. Again, each firm starts with R&D strategy equal to 0.0375.

It was already shown in Section 4 that the difference between these two parameters has big implications for selection pressure. Because the aggregate leverage ratio does not wander far from the neutral value, the leverage ratios of individual firms tend to be distributed in the vicinity of $\widetilde{\Omega}$. Then, if b^{lo} is just a bit larger than (or even equal to) $\widetilde{\Omega}$, relatively many firms will be vulnerable to bankruptcy. With a larger difference between the two parameters, fewer firms, namely, only those with the very highest leverage ratios are vulnerable.

The emerging heterogeneity that was discussed in Section 4.1, which implies the presence of stochastic 'noise' in the selection environment, plays a particularly salient role in these experiments. Due to stochasticity in the core Keynesian module (i.e., distributed multiplier mechanism) of the model, some bankruptcies will happen 'for no good reason', that is, without the firm having structural characteristics that make it less 'fit' than other firms. The likelihood of these types of bankruptcies is a decreasing function of the difference between parameters b^{lo} and $\widetilde{\Omega}$. However, $b^{lo} \gg \widetilde{\Omega}$ also implies less stringent selection to separate the wheat from the chaff, that is, this will also affect the macroeconomic viability of competing and heterogeneous R&D strategies. This is what motivates the interest in the specific simulations in this section.

In the first experiment, in Figure 19, we vary the neutral leverage ratio from 0.6 to 0.8 in steps of 0.02, and we set $b^{lo} = \widetilde{\Omega}$. Hence this is an experiment with high selection pressure. In the next experiments in this section, the neutral leverage ratio will be varied over the same range, but we set $b^{lo} = \widetilde{\Omega} + 0.1$ and $b^{lo} = \widetilde{\Omega} + 0.2$. In all experiments in this section, all firms start at R&D = 0.0375. The innovation mode is 1, and we set the fixed innovation step to 0.004. All other parameters are as in the table of the appendix (Appendix II).

Figure 19 shows the first experiment, with $b^{lo} = \widetilde{\Omega}$. We see that irrespective of the interest rate spread, R&D and growth are highest for a narrow band of low

Keynes–Schumpeter Macroeconomics

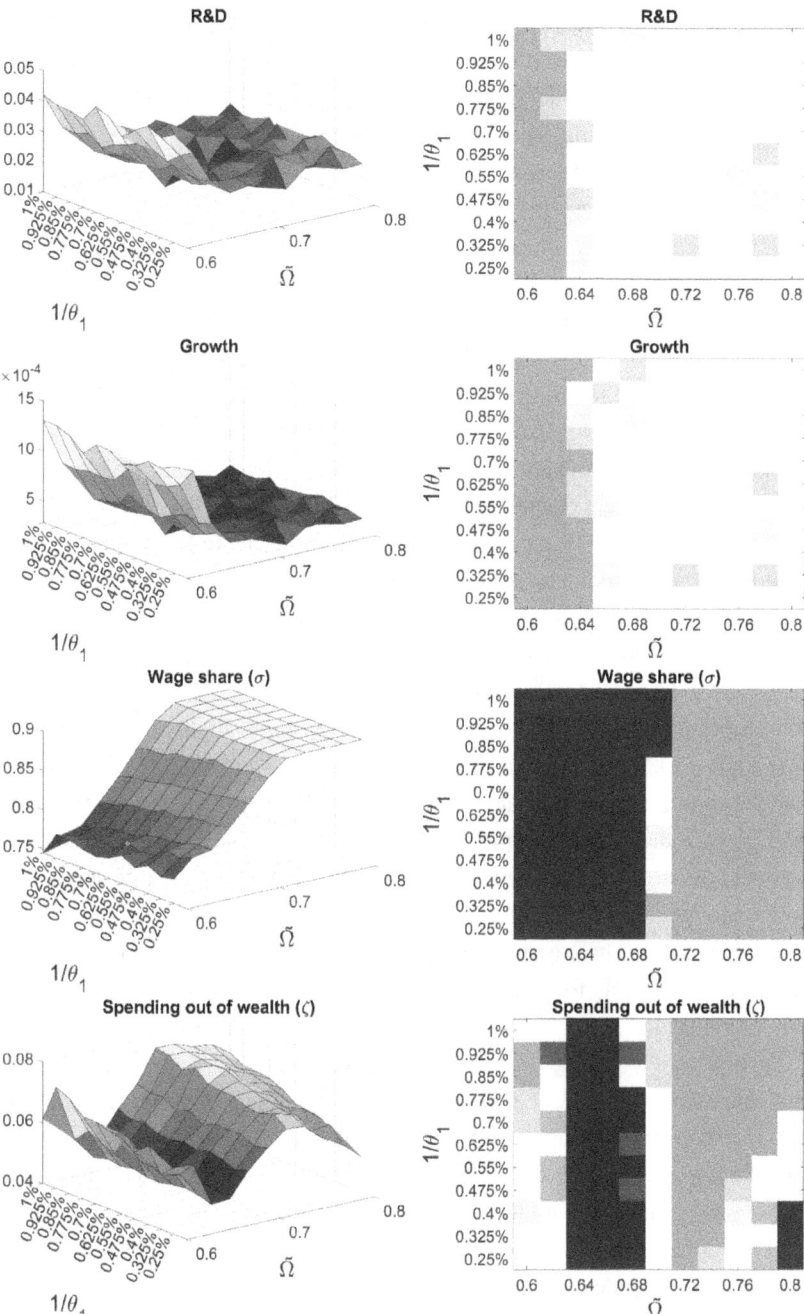

Figure 19 Varying the neutral leverage ratio ($\widetilde{\Omega}$) and minimum bankruptcy vulnerability ($b^{lo} = \widetilde{\Omega}$) against the interest rate parameter.

values for $\widetilde{\Omega}$. With values of this parameter equal to 0.6, only relatively high-R&D (approximately 4% of output) firms survive in the market. When $\widetilde{\Omega}$ rises, observed R&D levels quickly fall until they settle at around 2%. At $\widetilde{\Omega} = 0.66$ and beyond, R&D settles at around 2% of output.

The key to understanding this result is that R&D both increases productivity, which makes firms less indebted because their profit margin increases, and represents extra costs, which tends to increase firm indebtedness. Different levels of R&D spending will result in different levels of indebtedness (note that the productivity effect is nonlinear as in Figure 8). With $\widetilde{\Omega} = b^{lo} = 0.6$, firms spending less than 4% on R&D will tend to go bankrupt at a high rate because they do not realize sufficient productivity increases, and firms spending more will go bankrupt because the productivity increases they realize do not outweigh the extra R&D costs. With $\widetilde{\Omega}$ rising, these basic characteristics of the selection environment change to favour firms that spend less on R&D.

In the results for the wage share (σ), we see the familiar (e.g., from the steady-state analysis in Section 4) result that high R&D spending leads to low wage shares, because higher R&D costs must be compensated by lower wages for firms to remain close to the neutral leverage ratio. For very high values of $\widetilde{\Omega}$, the wage share hits the hard ceiling of 0.9 that is built into the model. For consumption spending out of wealth, the relationship is highly nonlinear.

In Figure 20, the experiment is repeated with $b^{lo} = \widetilde{\Omega} + 0.1$. In this case, we also see strong variations in the selection environment in the parameter space grid, but now the interest rate parameter also makes a difference. R&D is high in a broad corner of the parameter grid where $\widetilde{\Omega}$ and the interest rate spread are both relatively low. With high $\widetilde{\Omega}$, R&D is lower irrespective of the interest rate spread. The wage share and consumption spending out of wealth follow these movements, leading to widely varying values of these variables over the simulation grid.

Finally, in Figure 21, we set $b^{lo} = \widetilde{\Omega} + 0.2$. This changes the selection outcome again. Now R&D is low in the (broad) corner where the interest rate spread and $\widetilde{\Omega}$ are both high, with little significant variation elsewhere (except with the lowest interest rate spread, when R&D is high). Growth, the wage share and spending out of wealth follow this pattern.

Together, the experiments in this section show that the model endogenously generates R&D under a wide range of financial selection environments. Thus, R&D truly is an emergent property of the model, with the precise outcome in terms of R&D (and resulting effects on, among other things, growth, the functional income distribution and consumer wealth spending) difficult to predict in a precise sense by any equation that results from modelling individual

Keynes–Schumpeter Macroeconomics

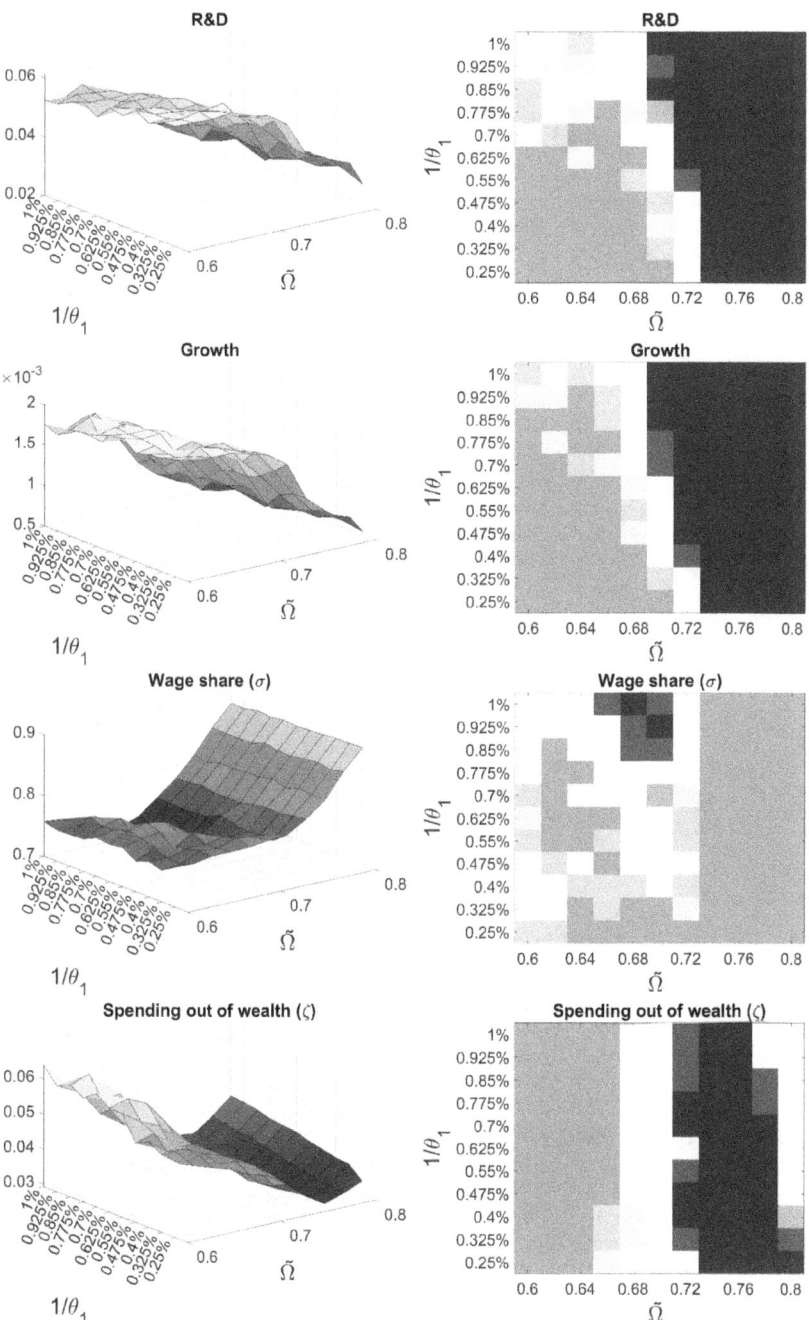

Figure 20 Varying the neutral leverage ratio ($\widetilde{\Omega}$) and minimum bankruptcy vulnerability ($b^{lo} = \widetilde{\Omega} + 0.1$) against the interest rate parameter.

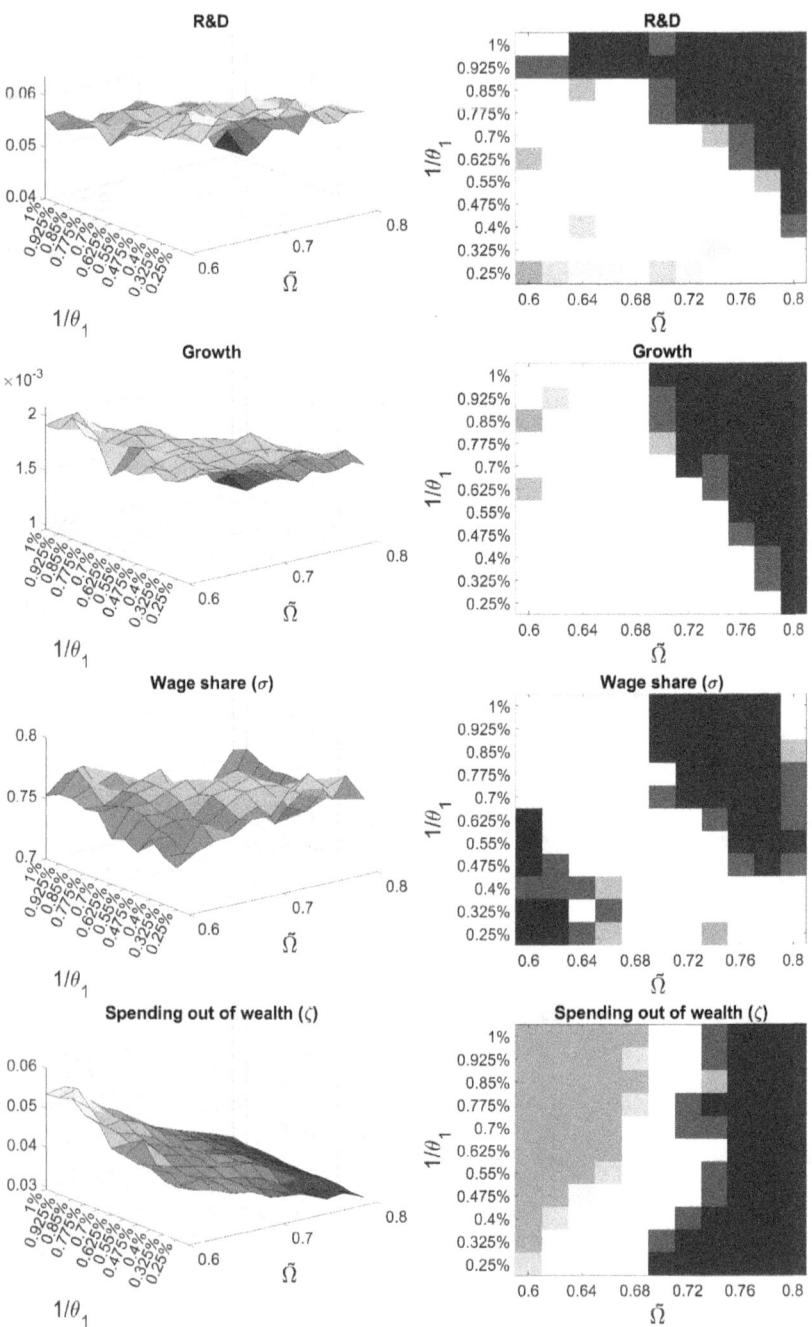

Figure 21 Varying the neutral leverage ratio ($\widetilde{\Omega}$) and minimum bankruptcy vulnerability ($b^{lo} = \widetilde{\Omega} + 0.2$) against the interest rate parameter.

agents. By tweaking the (financial aspects of the) selection environment, a wide variety of endogenous growth patterns can emerge.

5.5 Consumption

Next, we run two experiments that look at the influence of the (Keynesian) demand-side on R&D and growth, in particular consumption in the form of the marginal propensity to consume out of current-period income (wages and interest). We use innovation mode 2, with $\overline{P}^{mod2} = 0.5$ and vary $\widetilde{\varphi}$ between two experiments ($\widetilde{\varphi} = 0.006$ and 0.004). In the parameter grid, we keep the interest rate spread parameter θ_1 as one dimension and β, the propensity to consume out of wage income, as the other dimension. We vary β from 0.675 to 0.85 in steps of 0.0175. All other parameter values are as in the table of the appendix in Appendix II. As before, each firm starts with R&D strategy equal to 0.0375.

In Figure 22, there is only little influence from the change in β. Differences in R&D are not large across the parameter grid: it roughly varies between 5.5% and 6.5%. The lowest values occur with high interest rates, especially with high values of β. Most variation occurs in the results for the wage share and consumption out of wealth. The latter clearly offsets the effect of spending out of wage income: with high values for β, ζ tends to be lower. The wage share is lower for high-interest rate spreads, and low β. Interestingly, this suggests that high consumer spending, at least in terms of β, raises the wage income of households.

In Figure 23, technological opportunities are lower ($\widetilde{\varphi} = 0.004$), and this changes the outcomes considerably. R&D spending is generally lower, but with more variation across the grid. Minimum R&D spending is about 1.8% (this happens with high-interest rate spread and high β), while the maximum value (observed in the opposite corner with low β and low-interest rate spread) is about 4.6%. Thus, in this simulation, both high consumer spending (out of wages) and high-interest rate spreads crowd out R&D expenditures. Such crowding out results from the cash-flow equation of firms, where balancing different types of expenditures keeps the firm near the neutral leverage ratio. For the other variables, consumption spending again compensates for variations in β, but in this case variations in the wage share are mostly related to the interest rate spread.

The experiments in this section show that although the model has Keynesian features in the form of endogenous demand, this does not imply that demand has a positive impact on growth in the long run. Endogenous demand keeps demand in pace with productivity, but demand follows rather than leads. High demand may even crowd out R&D investment. In this sense, our model is clearly Schumpeterian rather than Keynesian.

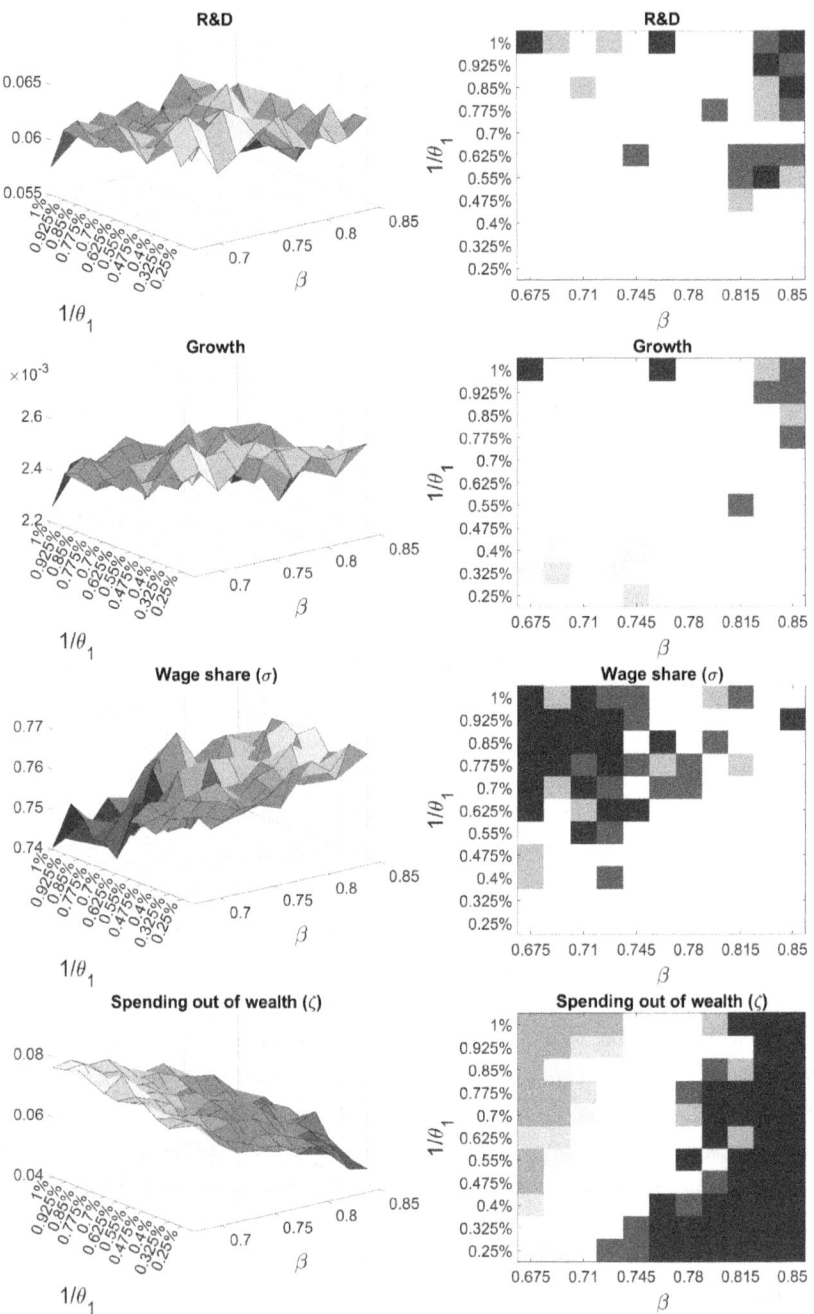

Figure 22 Varying the marginal propensity to consume out of wage income (β) against the interest rate parameter, innovation mode 2, $\widetilde{\varphi} = 0.006$.

Keynes–Schumpeter Macroeconomics

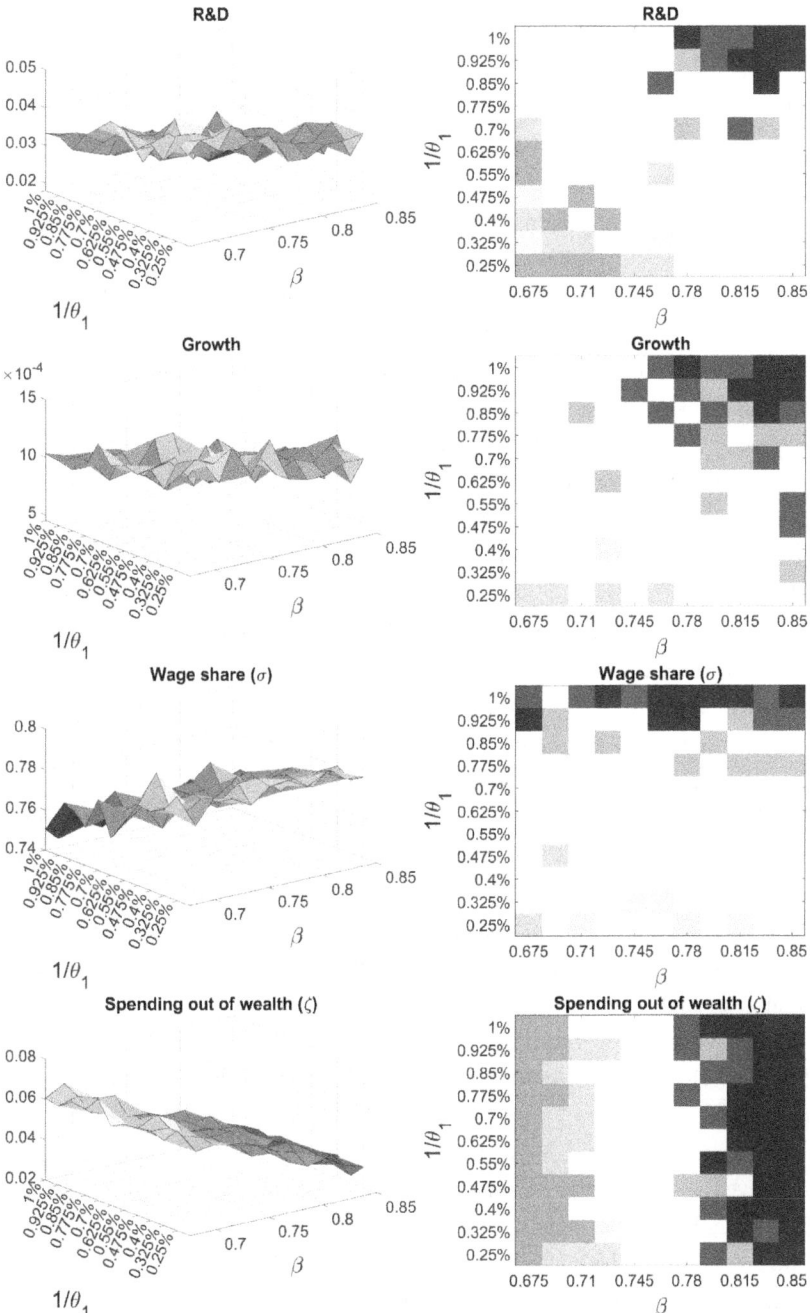

Figure 23 Varying the marginal propensity to consume out of wage income (β) against the interest rate parameter, innovation mode 2, $\widetilde{\varphi} = 0.004$.

5.6 Business Cycles with R&D and growth

Finally, we return to the topic of business cycles. Our main interest here is whether the nature of business cycles changes as a result of endogenous growth based on R&D. Therefore, we use the same experiment as in Section 3.8, that is, we vary the adjustment parameters α (for the share of household wealth spent on consumption, ζ) and φ, the parameter from the investment equation. These two parameters form the base grid of two experiments that vary β, the propensity to consume out of wage income (also used in the previous section). α varies from 0.005 to 0.025 in steps of 0.002, φ varies from 0.025 to 0.055 in steps of 0.003. The values for β that are used are 0.675 and 0.84. Firms invest in R&D with innovation mode 1, with fixed innovation step $\overline{\varphi}^{mod1} = 0.004$ and $\Phi^{mod1} = 6.667$. All other parameters are as in the table of the appendix (Appendix II).

Figure 24 shows the spectral decomposition results for $\beta = 0.675$. As in Section 3, these are averages of the spectral decomposition of 50 runs with identical parameters but different random seeds. The last 400 periods of a 1,000-period run were used for this Fourier analysis. The figure presents results for the four corners of the parameter grid (i.e., low/high α and low/high φ in all four possible combinations), as well as the centre of the parameter grid (middle values for α and φ).

These results are rather similar to those in Section 3, that is, without R&D and technological progress. For low values of α we see (very) long cycles, and with increasing α these cycles become shorter. In this case, the cycles for the lowest values of α are very long, up to the point that for low values of φ, the highest (average) density peaks at one cycle per 400 periods (i.e., a trend) when α is equal to 0.005 (the minimum value). This peak value is part of a range of high spectral density for 1–3 cycles.[13] Between 5 and 10 cycles per 400 periods are observed with low α and high φ (bottom-left and upper-right plots). Cycles grow shorter (up to 20 cycles per 400 periods) for higher values of α and φ.

When β is raised to 0.84, as in Figure 25, these basic results emerge again. However, in this case, a secondary cycle also emerges, with lower spectral density and shorter than the cycles in Figure 24. This is observed in the top- and middle-right, and the bottom-left sub-diagrams of Figure 24. Thus, it seems to be the case that a high value of the propensity to consume out of wage income can also contribute to (high-frequency) business cycles.

---

[13] We also did the Fourier analysis after removing a linear trend. This does not change the results much, although the peak density is now at 2 cycles rather than 1.

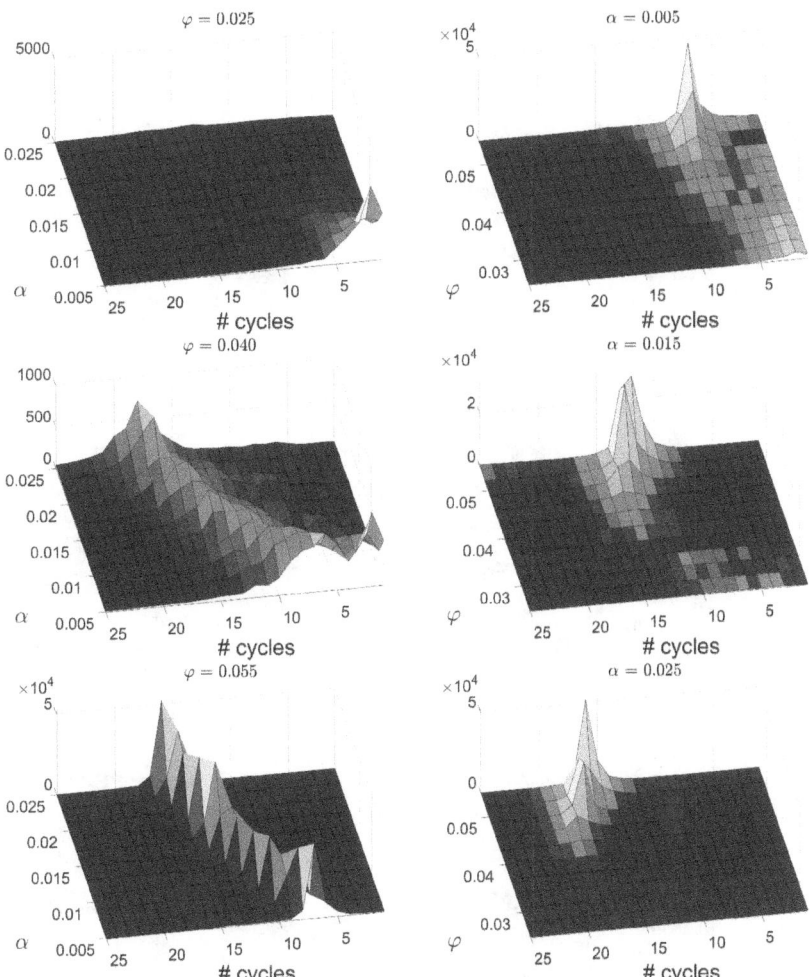

Figure 24 Fourier analysis of the employment rate in individual time series (spectral density on the Z-axis), $\beta = 0.675$.

Thus, we can conclude that the nature of business cycles does not change in any major way when we introduce endogenous innovation in the model. The Keynes–Schumpeter economy that we modelled shows fairly long business cycles largely independent of its growth rate.

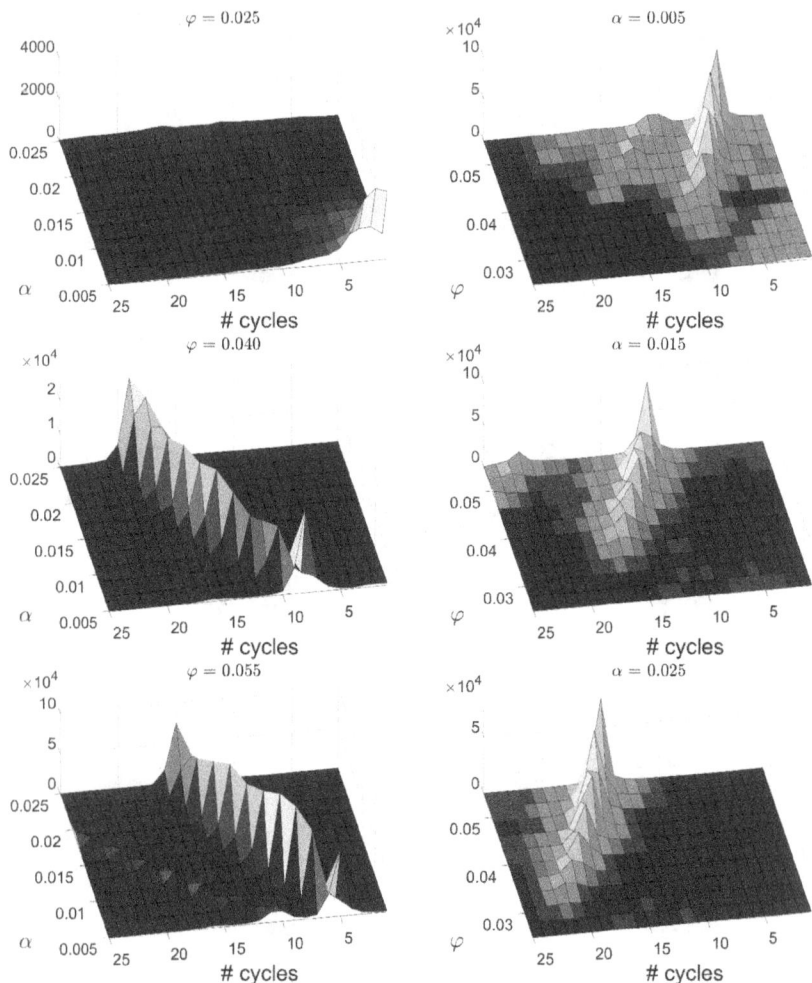

Figure 25 Fourier analysis of the employment rate in individual time series (spectral density on the Z-axis), $\beta = 0.84$.

6 Conclusions and Outlook

The Keynes–Schumpeter model that we proposed and analyzed in this Element portrays the macroeconomy as a disequilibrium process in which the demand-side and the supply-side are both endogenous. On the Schumpeterian side, innovation is endogenous through a selection process in which, under most parameter settings, an evolutionary stable R&D strategy emerges. This means that firms converge to a relatively narrow range of R&D strategies that remain stable, despite constant mutation of strategy.

R&D yields productivity growth, which implies a tendency for unemployment to grow under the pressure of replacement of labour. However, on the Keynesian side of the model, demand adjusts to keep the employment rate in a stable narrow range. This is achieved through a mechanism of consumption smoothing of households, which adjusts the fraction of their stock of financial wealth that they consume each period. The evolution of this stock of financial wealth is fully endogenous in a stock-flow-consistent (SFC) way. No government intervention is necessary to keep the growth of demand in line with the growth of productivity.

Our simulation experiments show that the evolutionary stable level of R&D strategies, and hence macroeconomic R&D spending and productivity growth, adjust to parameter settings. For example, we have shown that parameters related to the working of the bankruptcy, which is the main vehicle for the evolutionary selection of firms, affect the aggregate level of R&D spending, as do parameters related to how R&D spending influences innovation or parameters related to demand and saving. Also, other endogenous variables in the model, such as the real wage rate, consumer spending out of financial wealth, and investment, adjust under the influence of endogenous changes in R&D spending.

We have kept important parts of the model very simple, to make it as parsimonious as possible. Thus, the preceding characteristics and outcomes of the model emerge under a very minimalistic setting. For example, we have no explicit modelling of the financial market, we have no rationality (only blind mutation) with regard to the choice of R&D strategies by firms, and we have a very simple technology landscape describing an S-shaped relationship between R&D spending and productivity growth.

This means that there are many ways in which our model could be developed further. One way is by incorporating more elements from the SFC modelling tradition, which pays great attention to the details of the financial system. Our modelling of finance is crude, but financial mechanisms play a key role in the evolutionary selection mechanism that yields the evolutionary stable level of R&D spending. Incorporating (some of) the details of existing SFC models into our model will enrich both our modelling of evolutionary selection, and the supply side of SFC models, which usually have no endogenous R&D. This would provide a significant deepening of the Keynes–Schumpeter synthesis, and include an important element of current (post-)Keynesian modelling.

On the Schumpeterian side of our model, we see important potential for improving both the bounded rationality modelling of firms' decisions and of technology landscapes. On the latter, one relatively straightforward way would be to adopt NK landscapes or percolation landscapes as the representation of technological opportunities. This will provide a much richer set of possibilities for modelling the relationship between R&D spending and innovation, which could also include product innovation, instead of just productivity growth. However, with both NK landscapes and percolation landscapes, the problem of technological search (R&D) is essentially reduced to the trade-off between local search and the exploration of the landscape beyond the local environment.

This is an admittedly important facet of technological search, but bounded rationality of real-world R&D-performing firms also includes important other aspects. The key to using bounded rationality in evolutionary models like ours seems to be that firms must have truly different perceptions of the technology landscape and the economic system in which it is embedded. Thus, the way the technology landscape is modelled and the way bounded rationality can be operationalized seem to be closely connected. In a landscape where the only distinction is between local and global search, bounded rationality can only include this as a source of variation between firms.

The incorporation of NK landscapes into our model would allow the selection of firms on their boundedly rational R&D strategy in terms of local and global search. The outcome of the evolutionary selection process would then favour firms with a particular mix of local and global search. This would already be a major improvement compared to the 'completely blind' changes in firm strategy in our model. However, in reality, there are also other important aspects of the technology landscape and R&D and innovation strategies, for example, the relation between product and process innovation, possible complementarities between technologies, services innovation versus manufacturing innovation, the paradigmatic nature of technological change, and so on.

The inclusion of both a model of bounded rationality and of technological landscapes that would include many of these aspects is where we would like to see our model developing in the future.

Appendix I
The Steady State for a Notional Representative Agent

In this appendix, we will use a representative firm and household to investigate the dynamics of the aggregate leverage ratio. It should be noted that it is not straightforward to conceptualize a representative agent in the context of an agent-based model. In the exercise we present in this section, we assume a hypothetical steady state where, due to economic selection, all agents of the same type (be they firms or households) have converged to an identical state (regarding individual wealth/debt and behavioural variables such as the individual propensity to consume out of wealth, ζ_j, or firms' individual R&D strategy ρ_i), similar to the hypothetical case of an evolutionary stable symmetrical Nash equilibrium.

Under this assumption where none of the agents ever face bankruptcy (also implying that bond holders never face any wealth losses associated with bankruptcy), a representative agent can be understood as the aggregate of all the agents of its type. In this way, we will be able to derive exact mathematical expressions for the wage share σ and the share of wealth that is consumed, ζ. In the full model, as we simulate in Section 5 of the main text, such representative firms or households do not exist. As a result, the 'steady-state' expressions that we will derive in this appendix will not be observed in full simulations of the model. However, the equations that we will derive here give a much more precise indication of the trade-offs between important model variables that we derived in the main text, for example, between R&D and the wage share.

Before we get to the main part of the derivations, which are formed by the cash-flow equations of the representative firm and household, we look at capacity utilization, and the interest rate. The latter is determined in the financial market, and with additional simplifying assumptions, we can derive a simple expression for it. In particular, we assume that $\theta_0 = 1$, that the government interest rate $r^G = 0$, that, as a consequence, households do not want to hold any government bonds (they require $B/W = 1$), and also the sales tax rate is zero (because there are no government expenditures for which taxes need to be raised). Finally, we require that $B/W = 1$ is obtained as an 'interior solution'. This means that in terms of the equation for the interest rate spread that we introduced in the previous section, we have:

$$1 - \theta_0 + \theta_1\left(r^B - r^G\right) = \frac{B}{W} = 1 \to r^{B*} = \frac{1}{\theta_1}.$$

Note that we use the superscript * to denote a steady-state value.

For a steady-state capacity utilization rate u^*, it is required that the growth rate of output is equal to the growth rate of the capital stock. Dropping firm subscripts because we are looking at a single representative firm, denoting the growth rate of the capital stock as $\kappa_t \equiv (K_{t+1}/K_t) - 1$, and that of output as $g_t \equiv (Q_{t+1}/Q_t) - 1$, we must have $g^* = \kappa^*$. The equation (from the previous section) for the evolution of the capital stock then requires $I_t = (g^* + \delta)K_t$, while the investment plan made by firms implies $I_{i,t} = \delta K_{i,t-1} + K_{i,t-1}\varphi(u_{i,t-1} - \bar{u})$ (the growth rate is assumed to be positive, hence investment must also be positive). By equating these two expressions, we obtain

$$(g^* + \delta)K_t = \delta K_{i,t-1} + K_{i,t-1}\varphi(u_{i,t-1} - \bar{u}) \to u^* = \frac{(g^* + \delta)(1 + g^*) - \delta}{\varphi} + \bar{u}.$$

This says that the stable capacity utilization rate increases with the stable growth rate g^* in a quadratic fashion. This also enables us to find an expression for the stable investment-to-output ratio. With $K_t = Q_t v/u_t$ and $I_t = (g^* + \delta)K_t$, we easily obtain

$$\frac{I}{Q} = (g^* + \delta)\frac{v}{u^*}.$$

Now, it is time to return to the investigation of the implications of a stable leverage ratio. Using the forward difference $\Delta B_t \equiv B_{t+1} - B_t$, stability of the leverage ratio can be expressed as follows:

$$\frac{B_{t+1}}{K_{t+1}} \equiv \frac{B_t + \Delta B_t}{K_t(1 + \kappa_t)} = \frac{B_t}{K_t} = \widetilde{\Omega}.$$

Note that $\Lambda^* = \widetilde{\Omega}$. With the definitions for capacity utilization and the desired capital-output ratio that were formulated in the previous section, we have $Q_t = K_t u_t/v$. Together with the previous equation, this implies

$$\Delta B_t = K_t(1 + \kappa_t)\widetilde{\Omega} - B_t = K_t(1 + \kappa_t)\widetilde{\Omega} - \widetilde{\Omega}K_t = \widetilde{\Omega}\kappa_t Q_t \frac{v}{u_t}.$$

Now we must bring back the negative cash flow equation from the main text, this time explicitly denoting it as a forward difference:

$$\Delta B_t \equiv B_{t+1} - B_t = Q_{t+1}\sigma_{t+1} + I_{t+1} + \rho Q_t + r_t^B B_t - Q_{t+1}.$$

We equate the right-hand sides of the previous two equations, and substitute $I_{t+1} = (\kappa_{t+1} + \delta)K_{t+1}$, $B_t = \Lambda K_t$, $K_t = Q_t v/u_t$ and the steady-state values u^* and r^{B*} to yield

$$\widetilde{\Omega} g^* \frac{v}{u^*} = (1+g^*)\sigma_{t+1} + (g^* + \delta)\frac{v}{u^*}(1+g^*) + \rho + r^{B*}\widetilde{\Omega}\frac{v}{u^*} - (1+g^*).$$

This equation can be solved for the wage share σ, yielding the steady-state value for this variable:

$$\sigma^* = 1 - \frac{\frac{v}{u^*}\left((1 - \widetilde{\Omega} + g^* + \delta)g^* + \delta + r^{B*}\widetilde{\Omega}\right) + \rho}{1 + g^*}.$$

We can further substitute the steady-state value for u^*:

$$\sigma^* = 1 - \frac{v\varphi\left((1 - \widetilde{\Omega} + g^* + \delta)g^* + \delta + r^{B*}\widetilde{\Omega}\right)}{(g^* + \delta)(1+g^*)^2 + (\varphi\bar{u} - \delta)(1+g^*)} - \frac{\rho}{1+g^*}.$$

With our assumption that there are no government bonds because the government interest rate is zero, B_t also represents the wealth of the representative household, for which the cash flow equation is as follows:

$$\Delta B_t = Q_{t+1}(1 - c)\sigma_t - \zeta_t B_t + r_t B_t.$$

The basic logic of this equation is similar to the firm's cash-flow equation: we subtract the expenditures of the household in period $t + 1$ from income in the period, but note that in this case we do not use negative cash flows, as an increase in B_t represents an increase in wealth. The first term on the right-hand side represents the household's 'gross' savings, that is, wage income minus consumption out of wage. The second term is consumption out of wealth, which is autonomous consumption if seen from the aggregate point of view. The final term is interest income during the period.

Now we use $\Delta B_t = \widetilde{\Omega}\kappa_t Q_t v/u_t$ as derived earlier, and substitute steady-state values, including $B/K = \Lambda^* = \widetilde{\Omega}$, that were already obtained:

$$\widetilde{\Omega} g^* Q_t \frac{v}{u^*} = Q_{t+1}(1 - c)\sigma^* - \zeta_t Q_t \frac{v}{u^*}\widetilde{\Omega} + r_t Q_t \frac{v}{u^*}\widetilde{\Omega}.$$

From this, we can solve for a steady-state value for ζ:

$$\zeta^* = \frac{(1+g^*)(1-c)\sigma^*}{\frac{v}{u^*}\widetilde{\Omega}} + r_t - g^*.$$

Substituting the expression for u^*, this becomes

$$\zeta^* = \frac{\varphi(1+g^*)(1-c)\sigma^*}{v\widetilde{\Omega}\left((g^*+\delta)(1+g^*)-\delta+\varphi\bar{u}\right)} + r_t - g^*.$$

Wrapping up what we have found so far, we have two steady-state expressions, one for σ^* and one for ζ^*, with four unknowns: g^*, ρ, ζ^* and σ^* (r^{B*} has its own equation, that does not include any of the other steady-state values). This clearly leaves the system of two equations under-determined, but we have to consider one additional relationship, which is the one between ρ and g^*. This relationship is the topic of Section 4.3, where we specified two different innovation modes, which, in principle, could be combined.

Although it would be possible to use the representative firm framework to specify the relationship between ρ and g^* in an exact manner, we do not pursue this road, because the relation is non-linear and, therefore, would not yield easily interpretable relationships. It is clear, however, that increasing ρ will generally lead to an increasing g^*, under both innovation modes.

This leads to two further observations with respect to the steady-state expressions for ζ^* and σ^*. The first is that even if we take into account the relationship between ρ and g^*, the system is still under-determined, as we are one 'equation' short. This means that there is scope for multiple aggregate R&D strategies (ρ) to be consistent with the steady state with the representative firm and household. Which of these R&D strategies will prevail will ultimately depend on the selection process, and especially the imitation process, as described in Section 4.2. Of course, this is only relevant in the case with firm (and household) variety, as there is no selection with a single representative firm.

Second, because of the positive dependence of g^* on ρ, it is hard to see how σ^*, and therefore ζ^*, will change when ρ changes. In the steady-state expression, we see that the partial effect of a positive (negative) change in ρ will be to decrease (increase) σ^*. This makes intuitive sense because money that a firm spends on R&D cannot be spent on wages. Increasing (decreasing) σ^* will also have the partial effect of increasing (decreasing) ζ^*. However, the indirect effect of increasing ρ through g^* is difficult to grasp analytically, due to the complicated nature of the steady-state expressions. We explore those relationships numerically in the simulations in Section 5.2.

Appendix II
List of Variables, Parameters and Parameter Settings

Variable	Description
ς	Short-run utilization rate of a firm
W	Stock of monetary wealth of a household
ζ	Proportion of financial wealth spent on consumption (household level)
E	Fractional employment rate of a household
I	Investment of a firm
K	Capital stock of a firm
u	End-of-period capacity utilization rate of a firm
Q	Output of a firm
Q^K	Full-capacity output of a firm
R	R&D spending of a firm
B	Cumulative outstanding debt of (and bonds issued by) a firm
r^B	Interest rate paid by firms
Π	Operational surplus of a firm
b	Leverage ratio of the firm
a	Labour productivity of the firm
τ	Sales tax rate
Δ	Accumulated government deficit
B^G	Government bonds
C	Consumption
L	Employment
w	Wage rate
σ	Wage share of aggregate income
Λ	Aggregate leverage ratio

Note: firm-level or household-level variables can also be represented as weighted averages for aggregate versions.

Appendix II

Parameter	Description	Default value
ς^{min}	Lower capacity utilization limit for being chosen as seller	0.9
ς^{max}	Upper capacity utilization limit for being chosen as seller	1.1
γ	Batch size for transactions in the goods market	0.05
ϵ	Batch size for transactions in the labour market	0.01
ε	Maximum amount of work a household supplies	1.1
β	Marginal propensity to consume out of wage income	0.675
T^E	Number of periods that are remembered in the employment history	5
α	Adjustment parameter for ζ	0.02
$\overline{E}$	Target employment rate for households	0.95
δ	Rate of depreciation of physical capital	0.025
φ	Adjustment of investment to capacity utilization	0.025
ν	Capital coefficient, or normal capital-output ratio	8
r^G	Interest rate on government bonds	0.0025
θ_0	Interest rate bond preference parameter 0	1
θ_1	Interest rate bond preference parameter 1	Varying
b^{lo}	Lower bound of the positive bankruptcy window of the leverage ratio	0.6
b^{hi}	Higher bound of the positive bankruptcy window of the leverage ratio	2
bh^{lo}	Lower bound of the positive bankruptcy window of the household debt ratio	4
bh^{hi}	Higher bound of the positive bankruptcy window of the household debt ratio	5
χ	Bankruptcy debt liquidation	0.5
η	Capital loss in bankruptcy	0.2
$\tilde{b}$	Productivity lenience parameter 1 for bankruptcy	3
$\check{b}$	Productivity lenience parameter 2 for bankruptcy	0.9
$\check{d}$	Tax adjustment parameter	0.25
ϑ	Target public debt ratio for tax adjustment	0.9
τ^{max}	Maximum sales tax rate	0.6
σ^{lo}	Minimum admissible share of wages in income	0.4
σ^{hi}	Maximum admissible share of wages in income	0.9
$\overline{\Omega}$	Wage-setting parameter, max/min limit	1

Appendix II

(cont.)

Parameter	Description	Default value
$\breve{\Omega}$	Wage-setting parameter, base	0.15
$\tilde{\Omega}$	Wage-setting parameter, center	0.6
$\Omega^=$	Wage-setting parameter, exponent	1.5
π^{mut}	Fixed probability of mutation of the firm's R&D strategy (every period)	0.01
$imit$	Imitation mode parameter for labour productivity of a reborn firm	1
ρ^{up}	Upper limit for R&D strategy initialization and mutation of R&D strategy	0.075
B^{mut}	Bandwidth parameter for R&D strategy mutation	9
B^{imit}	Bandwidth parameter for R&D strategy imitation after bankruptcy	75
ϕ^{mod1}	Slope parameter for the innovation function in mode 1	2.5
ϕ^{mod2}	Slope parameter for the innovation function in mode 2	2.5
Φ^{mod1}	R&D efficiency parameter in mode 1	6.667
$\overline{\varphi}^{mod1}$	Fixed innovation step in mode 1	varying
$\overline{P}^{mod2}$	Innovation probability in mode 2	varying
$\tilde{\varphi}$	Maximum innovation step in mode 2	varying
$\tilde{A}$	Inflection point of the innovation efficiency function	3
ι	Minimum innovation efficiency (at Age = 0)	0.2
$\overline{A}$	Age parameter for selection of imitation target	1
n^{imit}	Number of imitation targets considered	5

References

Aghion, P. and P. Howitt (1992). A model of growth through creative destruction. *Econometrica* 60, 323–351. https://doi.org/10.2307/2951599.

Arestis, P. and M. Sawyer (2004). *The Post-Keynesian Approach to Economics*. Aldershot: Edward Elgar Publishing.

Berger, S. (ed.) (2009). *The Foundations of Non-Equilibrium Economics: The Principle of Circular and Cumulative Causation* (1st ed.). Milton Park, Abingdon-on-Thames: Routledge. https://doi.org/10.4324/9780203873731.

Caiani, A., Godin, A. and S. Lucarelli (2014). Innovation and finance: A stock flow consistent analysis of great surges of development. *Journal of Evolutionary Economics* 24, 421–448. https://doi.org/10.1007/s00191-014-0346-8.

Dosi, G. (1982). Technological paradigms and technological trajectories. *Research Policy* 11, 147–162. https://doi.org/10.1016/0048-7333(82)90016-6.

Dosi, G., Freeman, C., Nelson, R. R., Silverberg, G. and L. Soete (eds.) (1988). *Technical Change and Economic Theory*. London: Francis Pinter.

Dosi, G., Faggiolo, G. and A. Roventini (2010). Schumpeter meeting Keynes: a policy-friendly model of endogenous growth and business cycles. *Journal of Economic Dynamics and Control* 34, 1748–1767. https://doi.org/10.1016/j.jedc.2010.06.018.

Fagerberg, J. and B. Verspagen (2021). Technological revolutions, structural change, and catching up. In Foster McGregor, N., Alcorta, L., Szirmai, A. and B. Verspagen (eds.) *New Perspectives on Structural Change*. Oxford: Oxford University Press, pp. 131–155.

Freeman, C., Clark, J. and L. Soete (1982). *Unemployment and Technical Innovation: A Study of Long Waves and Technologies*. London: Frances Pinter.

Freitas, F. and F. Serrano (2015). Growth rate and level effects, the stability of the adjustment of capacity to demand and the Sraffian supermultiplier. *Review of Political Economy* 27, 258–281. DOI: https://doi.org/10.1080/09538259.2015.1067360.

Frenken, K. (2006). A fitness landscape approach to technological complexity, modularity, and vertical disintegration. *Structural Change and Economic Dynamics* 17, 288–305. https://doi.org/10.1016/j.strueco.2006.01.001.

Godley, W. and M. Lavoie (2007). *Monetary Economics: An Integrated Approach to Credit, Money, Income, Production and Wealth*. London: Palgrave Macmillan.

Hicks, J. R. (1937). Mr. Keynes and the 'Classics': A suggested interpretation. *Econometrica* 5, 147–159. https://doi.org/10.2307/1907242.

Hofbauer, J. and K. Sigmund (1998). *Evolutionary Games and Population Dynamics*. Cambridge, UK: Cambridge University Press.

Iwai, K. (1984a). Schumpeterian dynamics: An evolutionary model of innovation and imitation. *Journal of Economic Behaviour and Organization* 5, 159–190. https://doi.org/10.1016/0167-2681(84)90017-9.

Iwai, K. (1984b). Schumpeterian dynamics, Part II: Technological progress, firm growth and 'economic selection'. *Journal of Economic Behaviour and Organization* 5, 321–351. https://doi.org/10.1016/0167-2681(84)90005-2.

Keynes, J. M. (1936). *The General Theory of Employment, Interest, and Money*. London: Macmillan.

Langton, C. G. (1990). Computation at the edge of chaos: Phase transitions and emergent computation. *Physica D* 42, 12–37. https://doi.org/10.1016/0167-2789(90)90064-V.

Lorentz, A., Ciarli, T., Savona, M. and M. Valente (2016). The effect of demand-driven structural transformations on growth and technological change. *Journal of Evolutionary Economics* 26, 219–246. https://doi.org/10.1007/s00191-015-0409-5.

Maynard-Smith, J. (1974). The theory of games and the evolution of animal conflicts. *Journal of Theoretical Biology* 47, 209–221. https://doi.org/10.1016/0022-5193(74)90110-6.

Meijers, H., Nomaler, Ö. and B. Verspagen (2019). Demand, credit and macroeconomic dynamics: A micro simulation model. *Journal of Evolutionary Economics* 29, 337–364. https://doi.org/10.1007/s00191-018-0553-9.

Mensch, G. (1979). *Stalemate in technology: Innovations overcome the depression*. Cambridge, MA: Ballinger (translated from the German *Das Technologische Patt*. Frankfurt: Umschau, 1975).

Nelson, R. R. and S. G. Winter (1982). *An Evolutionary Theory of Economic Change*. Cambridge, MA: The Belknap Press.

Nomaler, Ö., Spinola, D. and B. Verspagen (2021). R&D-based economic growth in a supermultiplier model. *Structural Change and Economic Dynamics* 59, 1–19. https://doi.org/10.1016/j.strueco.2021.07.002.

Pasinetti, L. (2007). *Keynes and the Cambridge Keynesians: A 'Revolution in Economics' to be Accomplished*. Cambridge, UK: Cambridge University Press.

Prigogine, I. and I. Stengers (1984). *Order Out of Chaos: Man's New Dialogue with Nature*. New York, NY: Bantam Books.

Robinson, J. (1937). *Introduction to the Theory of Employment*. London: Macmillan.

Romer, P. (1990). Endogenous Technological Change. *Journal of Political Economy* 98, Part 2, S71–S102. https://doi.org/10.1086/261725.

Schumpeter, J. A. (1911). *Theorie der wirtschaftlichen Entwicklung*. Leipzig: Duncker & Humblot.

Schumpeter, J. A. (1948). Science and ideology. *The American Economic Review* 39, 346–359.

Silverberg, G. (1988). Modelling economic dynamics and technical change: Mathematical approaches to self-organisation and evolution. In Dosi et al. (eds.), 531–595.

Silverberg, G., Dosi, G. and L. Orsenigo (1988). Innovation, diversity and diffusion: A self-organisation model. *Economic Journal* 98, 1032–1054. https://doi.org/10.2307/2233718.

Silverberg, G. and B. Verspagen (1994). Learning, innovation and economic growth: A long-run model of industrial dynamics. *Industrial and Corporate Change* 3, 199–223. https://doi.org/10.1093/icc/3.1.199.

Silverberg, G. and B. Verspagen (2005). A percolation model of innovation in complex technology spaces. *Journal of Economic Dynamics and Control* 29, 225–244. https://doi.org/10.1016/j.jedc.2003.05.005.

Taylor, L. (2020). *Reconstructing Macroeconomics: Structuralist Proposals and Critiques of the Mainstream*. Cambridge, MA: Harvard University Press.

Tesfatsion, L. (2002). Agent-based computational economics: Growing economies from the bottom up. *Artificial Life* 8, 55–82. https://doi.org/10.1162/106454602753694765.

Valente, M. (2014). An NK-like model for complexity. *Journal of Evolutionary Economics* 24, 107–134. https://doi.org/10.1007/s00191-013-0334-4.

Cambridge Elements

Evolutionary Economics

John Foster
University of Queensland

John Foster is Emeritus Professor of Economics and former Head of the School of Economics at the University of Queensland, Brisbane. He is Fellow of the Academy of Social Science in Australia, Life member of Clare Hall College, Cambridge and Past President of the International J.A. Schumpeter Society.

Jason Potts
RMIT University

Jason Potts is Professor of Economics at RMIT University, Melbourne. He is also an Adjunct Fellow at the Institute of Public Affairs. His research interests include technological change, economics of innovation, and economics of cities. He was the winner of the 2000 International Joseph A. Schumpeter Prize and has published over 60 articles and six books.

Isabel Almudi
University of Zaragoza

Isabel Almudi is Professor of Economics at the University of Zaragoza, Spain, where she also belongs to the Instituto de Biocomputación y Física de Sistemas Complejos. She has been Visiting Fellow at the European University Institute, Columbia University and RMIT University. Her research fields are evolutionary economics, innovation studies, environmental economics and dynamic systems.

Francisco Fatas-Villafranca
University of Zaragoza

Francisco Fatas-Villafranca is Professor of Economics at the University of Zaragoza, Spain. He has been Visiting Scholar at Columbia University and Visiting Researcher at the University of Manchester. His research focuses on economic theory and quantitative methods in the social sciences, with special interest in evolutionary economics.

David A. Harper
New York University

David A. Harper is Clinical Professor of Economics and Co-Director of the Program on the Foundations of the Market Economy at New York University. His research interests span institutional economics, Austrian economics and evolutionary economics. He has written two books and has published extensively in academic journals. He was formerly Chief Analyst and Manager at the New Zealand Treasury.

About the Series

Cambridge Elements of Evolutionary Economics provides authoritative and up-to-date reviews of core topics and recent developments in the field. It includes state-of-the-art contributions on all areas in the field. The series is broadly concerned with questions of dynamics and change, with a particular focus on processes of entrepreneurship and innovation, industrial and institutional dynamics, and on patterns of economic growth and development.

Cambridge Elements

Evolutionary Economics

Elements in the Series

A Reconsideration of the Theory of Non-Linear Scale Effects: The Sources of Varying Returns to, and Economics of, Scale
Richard G. Lipsey

Evolutionary Economics: Its Nature and Future
Geoffrey M. Hodgson

Coevolution in Economic Systems
Isabel Almudi and Francisco Fatas-Villafranca

Industrial Policy: The Coevolution of Public and Private Sources of Finance for Important Emerging and Evolving Technologies
Kenneth I. Carlaw and Richard G. Lipsey

Explaining Technology
Roger Koppl, Roberto Cazzolla Gatti, Abigail Devereaux, Brian D. Fath, James Herriot, Wim Hordijk, Stuart Kauffman, Robert E. Ulanowicz and Sergi Valverde

Evolutionary Games and the Replicator Dynamics
Saul Mendoza-Palacios and Onésimo Hernández-Lerma

The Dynamic Metacapabilities Framework: Introducing Quantum Management and the Informational View of the Firm
Harold Paredes-Frigolett and Andreas Pyka

Entrepreneurship and Evolutionary Economics
Per L. Bylund

Agent-Based Macroeconomics: The Schumpeter Meeting Keynes Models
Giovanni Dosi and Andrea Roventini

Evolutionary Price Theory
Harry Bloch

Institutional Acceleration: The Consequences of Technological Change in a Digital Economy
Darcy W. E. Allen, Chris Berg and Jason Potts

Evolutionary Selection and Keynes–Schumpeter Macroeconomics
Önder Nomaler, Danilo Spinola and Bart Verspagen

A full series listing is available at: www.cambridge.org/EEVE

Printed by Integrated Books International,
United States of America